T0193105

# INNINGS

MIKE ROBERTSON

authorHOUSE®

*AuthorHouse™*
*1663 Liberty Drive*
*Bloomington, IN 47403*
*www.authorhouse.com*
*Phone: 1 (800) 839-8640*

*Published by AuthorHouse  03/27/2019*

*ISBN: 978-1-7283-0526-4 (sc)*
*ISBN: 978-1-7283-0525-7 (hc)*
*ISBN: 978-1-7283-0524-0 (e)*

*Library of Congress Control Number: 2019903449*

*Print information available on the last page.*

# LONGTIME GONE

*I kept statistics, took notes, and wrote commentaries about the travails of practically every recreational baseball team on which I have ever played. This custom, which most of my friends, including my long suffering wife, considered pathological though harmless, began about the time I was introduced to the adventures of little league. I am not alone in recording such chronicles, noting that hundreds of books have been written and dozens of motion pictures produced about baseball. However, my chronology, as humble as it is, does not involve any particular instances of tragedy or triumph, only sixty years of playing various forms of recreational ball.*

While I cannot be certain, the misfortunes of a receding memory taking its toll, I think my captivation with the game of baseball began sometime in the late 1950s. Like the origins of most pursuits, my interest in baseball started accidentally, as if my eventual obsession with the sport was not destined but simple fortune, like a roll of the dice in some region of heaven. I had happened to start collecting baseball cards, not out of my curiosity in the sport itself but in the use to which some of my classmates had put the cards. It was mainly the pursuit of competitively flinging the cards against walls or fences in schoolyard contests with childish names like farthies, toppers, and leaners. Initially, I had not pay much attention to the card games, engaged as I was in various other recreations, mainly physical activities like Red Rover, British Bulldog, Cops and Robbers, Dodge Ball, and a barely recalled game called Stand-Still. I had also occasionally played major schoolyard recreations like hockey, football and baseball but the latter three seemed not quite as appealing to me as the other, less well known games. At the time I concluded, perhaps as an excuse as opposed to an explanation, that my lack of enthusiasm for those three major sports was based on my opinion, at least at the time, that they had an unhealthy dependence on rules and standards, the latter often acting as a measurement of my own limitations as a participant.

As for the card games, I was initially reluctant about them as well. They seemed reserved for nerds, nervous looking little boys who only came out of their shells with a pack of hockey, football or baseball cards in their furtive little hands. They weren't exactly serious collectors although I'm sure some of them may have been. The specific game didn't really matter although I was fairly certain that everyone had their own preferences. At first, I casually loitered around such games. I gradually came to spectate with more than just curiosity. I began to spend more time at the games, investing my recesses and most of my lunch periods in hanging around them. As a consequence, I began to shun most, if not all of the previously pursued schoolyard recreations. I still didn't know why. My friends, many of whom were initially merciless in disapproving of my new diversion, began to encourage me to participate in the card games rather than simply watching them. I started as a pick up man for a relatively mediocre player named Tommy and within a week or so, I was on the line playing toppers against a variety of opponents, many of whom were surprisingly agreeable in allowing me to participate in their games.

For reasons that I probably could never explain, even to myself, I quickly become proficient at such games, eventually amassing an impressive stack of cards of various pedigrees, including, most particularly, baseball cards. Aside from the minor celebratory status I managed to attain among the group of card collecting dweebs, I had also developed a healthy interest in the actual cards that I was winning, most of which happened to be baseball cards. While I had always had a moderate interest in the game, participation in a host of schoolyard, street and backyard wiffle pickup games having left their effect, I was not terribly enthusiastic about baseball, preferring the joys of hockey, it being practically a patriotic duty for any ten year old boy living in Montreal, Quebec.

But the acquisition of a large collection of baseball cards eventually prompted a real interest in the sport itself. In fact, after another kid, no doubt a serious collector himself, offered me fifty cards for a 1958 Mickey Mantle card, which someone had acquired and then lost in a game of "toppers", baseball became more than just a casual interest to me.

# INNINGS

It became, like many boys my age, a preoccupation that was to survive well into my adult life. There was no other sensible explanation for the evolution of my interest in baseball. Still, I remained reasonably certain that a lot of other boys my age shared the same confusion regarding their fascination with baseball.

I was ten years old when I pestered my father, a notorious skinflint, into buying me a cheap though serviceable baseball glove. I began to practice my fielding by tossing a rubber ball against the brick siding of the family house. Unfortunately, my mother worked the night shift as a nurse at a local hospital and, therefore, was not happy when my fielding practice made so much noise as she was trying to get some much needed sleep. She would yell at me, I would stop practice for fifteen minutes or so and then continue to practice after I was convinced that she had resumed slumber, the only adjustment being that I started to throw the ball onto the roof. As for batting practice, I would organize games of wiffle ball, where the neighbourhood kids and I would swing a plastic bat, attempting to hit a bald tennis ball out of my backyard. My mother, not to mention my father and most of the neighbours, were not too happy with these games either, particularly when one of us would swat a home run over the hedge into an adjoining yard. This would precipitate a mild celebration and then a mad search for the ball, a possible apology to an angry neighbour, a lost tennis ball, and/or all of the above.

# FIRST SPRING

The next spring, now eleven years old, with a dollar advanced reluctantly by my still stingy father, I registered with the local community association for participation in the local little league. The local teams, including the little league, played their home games in Valois Park. It was a large field on which sat three baseball diamonds, the best facility of the three being equipped with lights, dugouts, outfield fences, and plenty of seating. Within a week, I was assigned to one of six house league teams, house league being the minor leagues for the city team, which was supposed to be comprised of the best players. My team was sponsored by the local pharmacy, the imperious Johnson's Drugstore, my only familiarity with which was the fact that it operated a soda fountain in the rear of the store.

I remember nervously reporting to the team's first practice. It was the second Saturday of May I think. I was given a green and white jersey with the name of the store emblazoned across the chest. Most of my new teammates were unknown to me, the only exceptions being one guy with whom I had played hockey the previous winter and two others who were in the same fifth grade class as I was in the Saint John Fisher elementary school, which just happened to be situated two blocks directly north of park. The team manager was a gruff old man named Pete Something-or-Other who liked to yell a lot and was constantly chomping on an unlit cigar when he wasn't smoking unfiltered cigarettes. The story, at least according to a couple of the guys in grade seven, was that Pete had played professional baseball in the minor leagues, for whom and where never having been revealed, at least to me. When I enthusiastically informed my father of this intriguing little fact, he just shrugged, my conclusion being that playing minor league baseball to my father was hardly the impressive accomplishment I thought it was. I should have anticipated his reaction, having listened to the old man knock my admiration for various members of the Montreal Canadiens, not to mention my own nascent pee wee hockey career. Decades later, he was still dismissing any kind of endeavour, regardless of whether I was pursuing, appreciating it or watching athletics on television.

That first season of playing organized baseball provided me with evidence of my own skills as a player, abilities which were arguably and relatively acceptable. Understandably, that experience required an adjustment from my previous baseball education in the schoolyard, backyard, and street games I had played over the previous few years. Organized baseball introduced me to all sorts of previously unknown habits: teams were not freshly assembled every time a game was played; players were required to wear t-shirts, if not uniforms; there were managers guiding the teams; there were umpires adjudicating over the games according to a complex sets of rules; there were team standings; there were people keeping score and compiling statistics; and at the end of the season, there were banquets during which trophies were distributed to deserving teams and players. Remember, this was the early 1960s, back when parents were not so spellbound with their kids' athletic endeavours. Fact was that parents seldom attended their kids' games in those days, particularly at the house league level where athletic ability was irrelevant, the only requirement being the payment of the registration fee of one dollar. In summary, this was a time when kids played baseball and other sports without the participation of their parents, the only adults involved being grouchy retreads like Pete the Manager and community scions who sponsored the teams.

After maybe three or four games, I came to the conclusion that I was one of the better players on the team, many of my teammates appearing to be tragically unfamiliar with the basics of the game. Not surprisingly, this caused poor Pete the Manager to yell himself hoarse in constant conniption, cigarette smoke and profanity circling him like a nimbus. Many of my teammates seemed genuinely terrified of Pete, a condition which hardly improved their already unfortunate play on the field. It turned out that I was one of the four or five members of the team who played competently enough to avoid Pete's wrath. I, therefore, did not fear Pete although I always thought that I was a botched fly ball or pathetic strike out away from infamy and a seat on the bench, the bench being the immortal "pine" where the lousy players sat out their tenure on the team like prisoners awaiting trial. On this point, throughout my decades as first a player and then as a manager, I had always struggled with the question of so-called bench players, guys who weren't useful enough to play regularly but were needed nonetheless to ensure that nine players could be fielded. On that first little league team, there were four or five kids who had a tentative grasp on the game, their only qualifications it seemed was the fact that they were boys of the right age, had paid their fees and owned baseball gloves. Anyway, even crusty old Pete the Manager seemed to have misgivings about their fates, sometimes playing them, particularly when the game was out of hand either way, sometimes having them sit out the entire game, which at least two of them didn't seem to mind, and the others apparently unhappy but unwillingly it seemed to complain. Years later, when I was managing my own team, I would reflect on that general question on many occasions. Even then, not to mention now, benching any player on any recreational team seemed absurd, if not cruel.

That year, I think the Johnson's Drug team finished second in the house league, losing eventually to PC Lemaire, a small construction company. The other teams in that house league were Hub Hardware, Fraser Sports, Laviolette's Grocery and Helen's Taxi, the latter owned and operated by a middle aged woman who some of the players claimed could have been married to Pete the Manager, their resemblance to each other the main reason. I thought that I might have hit .400 that first year, to me an astounding batting average given that a player named Dick Groat of the Pittsburgh Pirates led the major leagues with a batting average of .325. The house league did not, however, compile batting statistics, my batting average calculated by yours truly, after one of my classmates, a boy named Teddy McMahon, boasted that he had hit over .500 for Hub Hardware. That September, after the house league season was over, we had gotten into a schoolyard dispute about the matter. For some reason, being eleven years old may have had something to be with it, I felt compelled to prove, at least to myself, that I could have hit .500 myself. But, how I thought about it. While I considered the conundrum for a day or so, I knew I had to disapprove Teddy McMahon's claim. Although I may not have actually cared too much about personalities at the time, I did dislike him. Like a lot of my classmates, I considered him somewhat of a bully. Besides, it was a matter of juvenile honour. Sort of.

I'll admit now, although not at the time, that it was dumb but I went ahead about correcting McMahon's assertions anyway, at least in my day dreams. I spent the last month of my summer vacation that year fantasizing the assembly of what would amount to be my own batting statistics for the season that had just concluded. Sure, I felt weird thinking about it. I knew that but I felt obligated, as if I was addicted somehow to recording my own triumphs, a preoccupation that I later found out wasn't that unusual. Regarding the latter observation, over the years, as I continued to participate in other leagues and in other sports, I became aware of many other players who compiled their own statistics. In fact, some were even egocentric enough to collect and maintain data on any athletic game they had played, regardless of the level of competition. Some even included pick up games played in school yards and empty parks. One boy I knew claimed to have complete information on the number of goals he had scored during street hockey games while another said that he had kept statistics on a baseball board game called Strat-O-Matic that he and his three brothers had regularly played. It made me feel better to know that there were other kids who were as compulsive as I was when it came to their own stats. For a while, I had thought that I was going nuts, but I wasn't, at least not then. On the other hand, adolescence was fast approaching. Then I would really find out about going nuts. My ambition regarding the discovery of my own baseball statistics turned into a full time fantasy. I thought it might have gone like the following, a day dream that preoccupied an eleven year old throughout that summer.

Then there was my dream. Maybe it was my imagination.

*After discussing my ambition with some of my friends and even my father, who offered me a brusque little sneer and then went back to his paper, I decided to contact the little league commissioner, a man named Nolan who owned the local hardware store, Hub Hardware. I remember that it must have taken me a few days or so to actually identify and locate Mr. Nolan, repeated questioning of Old George, the creepy long time custodian of the Valois Park clubhouse, the first source to suggest his name. From there, I quickly found out that not only did Mr. Nolan happen to underwrite one of the teams in the baseball little league, the aforementioned Hub Hardware, but he was also sponsored one of the teams in the local Pop Warner football league, and park teams in both the pee wee and bantam hockey leagues. Everyone I spoke to, a couple of teachers and my own father, saw him as a pillar of the community. Mr. Nolan was relatively easy to find, even for an eleven year boy with a quixotic quest regarding little league baseball statistics. I approached him at a Pop Warner game maybe a month after the baseball season was over, he being pointed out to me by one of my classmates. I asked him, having rehearsed my spiel for maybe a week, for any score sheets the house league could provide, specifically as they may have pertained to the Johnson Drug team. After asking me to repeat my request, Mr. Nolan said that he would see what he could do, continually shaking his head and gently laughing. He told me to come by the hardware store the next week.*

*Three days later, I went down to Hub Hardware on Donegani Road. Mr. Nolan, who was dressed in a suit and tie just like my old man, appeared from the back of the store, handed me a batch of handwritten score sheets covering 16 of the 18 games that Johnson Drug had played that season. Ignoring the two games that were missing — I considered but didn't try to research my own memory — I painstakingly assembled my own stats, calculating that I had hit .425, well below the unverified .500 mark of Ted McMahon. I was disappointed, but as my friends pointed out, I definitely knew that I had hit .425, which was likely proficient enough to maybe place me among the team's, if not the league's better hitters. The league did not, however, compile, let alone distribute such information, its own official statistics being the scores of the games, final standings and playoff results, all of which were conveniently published in the local Lakeshore News. While I felt pretty good about that, I was careful not to advertise it. I suspected that my friends and teammates, who were aware of my investigation of my own statistics, were possibly ready to consider me an egotistic jerk. So I let the matter slide, deflecting all inquiries by claiming that I couldn't locate the numbers, hoping that Mr. Nolan was not consulted. In time, the matter was forgotten by pretty well everyone but myself.*

It could have happened. Maybe.

It was my first year of playing competitive baseball and my first year of thinking about compiling statistics regarding the performance of myself and others. In addition to thinking about assembling my own statistics, I decided, for a reason of which I am not sure, that I would write the story of that season, if not only for my own entertainment but as a response to a class assignment in composition class, the banal requirement for an account of my activities during the summer vacation, the traditional theme of "What I Did On My Summer Vacation". My story took the form of a series of thumbnail sketches of each of my teammates, including myself: boys with names like Baxter, Carter, Fitzpatrick, Gibson, Gogarty, Jackson, Lawrence, McDonald, Miller, Russell, and Waldron. All the character commentaries attempted to be more amusing than factual, although most if not all of them possessed enough fact to render them with some measure of accuracy. Reviewing them decades later, they seemed genuinely naive and stupidly comic as any narrative produced by any eleven year old trying to entertain himself. I had even considered not submitting the story in composition class but eventually decided to potentially allow my teammates to share my impressions of them. But they never got the chance as the stories were never distributed to the rest of the class, my mark of "A" and the comment "Funny" written by my sixth grade teacher, Mr. French, on the front page of my paper. Otherwise, my paper was filed away in a box with my baseball cards, my report cards, some photographs, and other historical relics only to be found decades later as a source for this current history.

The next spring, I tried out for the local city little league team, the Valois Yankees, having decided that it was worth a shot. I had already been guaranteed a spot on a house league team if I didn't make the city team, the former acting as a kind of de facto minor leagues for the city team. It was an inter-squad game. I played third base and left field. I figured I was regarded rather lightly but I guessed that I probably still had an outside chance, like maybe a dozen other nervous aspirants who had showed up for the tryouts that Saturday morning in May. Waiting for my turn at the plate during that game, as I was kneeing in the on-deck circle, I glanced out at the pitcher carefully. He seemed to me to be a magnificent figure, foreboding, full of menace and danger. I waited, looking out past him, past the infielders leaning forward with their hands on their knees, and into the outfield. Then looking at the coach with the chipboard and a whistle, I was almost prepared to genuflect, my fate in his hands I guess. I just waited, holding a bat and waiting as the pitcher tried to scare the batter with an occasional throw to the screen. And then, someone would somehow make contact, the ball suddenly sailing through the air like a miracle, and the batter would pause a moment to regard his work and then run out it out until the right fielder caught the ball he had just hit for an out. Then my opportunity came. I looked up. The sky was almost white, like an ocean about to erupt. A wind began to swirl. It was going to rain. The pitcher appeared perturbed. He glowered. He looked like he was prepared to remove my head. Or so I thought.

On the first pitch, after waiting nervously in the batter's box for maybe five seconds before the first pitch was delivered, I somehow managed, like the kid that had just batted before me, to actually hit the ball, this time walloping the ball over the right fielder's head. I didn't know how. It was pure luck I suppose. I was composed enough to actually follow the flight of the ball. I saw the right fielder's expression, bewildered and desperate, just a moment before he turned and gave chase. By this time, when I realized that some miracle of a golden glove was not about to appear out of the trees that circumscribed the field to catch the ball, I knew. It was a dead shot into the third deck. I was tempted to throw my arms up but didn't. I just started to run down the first base line, head down. I just thought I had been suddenly transformed into a star but was unfamiliar with the feeling. I felt embarrassed, too modest to celebrate unduly. I passed first base, noticed that the first baseman looked dumbfounded, as if he didn't know where to look. Confusion did not seem to confound the second baseman who was staring into right field, waving his arms and yelling. I started to head toward third base, the prospect of an actual home run was now perceptible.

I now imagined Mantle completing the journey around the bases, casually majestic, unhurried movements, seemingly unaware of the tumult around him. Of course, Mantle had almost certainly hit the ball over the fence, not compelled to complete the tour around the bases while an outfielder chased the ball. There was no need for Mantle to exert himself. He ran the bases like he was jogging through a park, a thoroughbred entering the winner's circle. He would touch the plate casually, without ceremony. There was no excessive celebration, in presumed deference to his opponents, the absence of histrionics an integral characteristic of the game back then, something that no longer seems to occur in the modern game, the bat flip and similar demonstrations of triumph now prevalent, if not required. Not having hit the ball over the fence — fact was that the Valois Park baseball diamond had a deep fence — I had to run out my home run, crossing the plate without a throw as I scored. There was no hint of error. It was a legitimate home run. Strangely and surprisingly, I was not saluted by my teammates on my arrival at the bench after the homer. There were no cheers, no coach to slap me on the back, no handshakes, fist bumps and high fives greetings yet to be introduced into the drama of athletics. As I stepped on the plate, I looked at the catcher. He was expressionless, almost as if he was unaware of my accomplishment. I glanced over my shoulder, the pitcher had turned away, staring into the outfield. Even the crowd, which was sparse, if not non-existent, was silent. After all, theses were inter-squad games. Had I launched a ball into the pastures of imagination? Was I dreaming? Was I imagining something off the backs of those baseball cards I had managed to acquire over the past year or so?

In my concern with the consequences of my good fortune, I had not noticed, my head down in an attempt to control my exultation, that someone had fallen down during the chase for the ball I had just hit. Most of the team in the field had immediately given up the ball for gone and had circled their fallen teammate as he lay face down in the outfield grass. The other team's coach administered to the boy as best as he could, examining him, picking him up and carrying him to his car. The practice game was called off. I felt like I would eventually be blamed somehow, and my home run, while it could have provided me with a reason to smirk for the remainder of the day, was forgotten. Besides, it was now raining.

As for the boy who had fallen down, the trauma was not serious enough to keep him out of the starting lineup for opening day the next week, a tender knee the reported injury. He was to play third base and bat fifth while I was exiled to left field and bat last, an eventuality which I interpreted as some sort of punishment. But I was not particularly gloomy. After all, I had made the team and the starting lineup. I hadn't expected it when I first showed up for tryouts.

It was opening day. There were flags, a parade and the sun was high in a deep blue sky. There was not a cloud anywhere, everything was civic pomp and circumstance. Another season was starting. It was the third Saturday in May 1961. There was quite a respectable crowd in attendance for that first day, a few town big shots were sitting in the stands with their wives, every player from both the Valois Yankees and our opponents, the Pointe Claire Pirates, might well have had a parent spectating that day, including my father. A priest threw out the first pitch and there was actually a public address announcer for the game. This was one big deal. It was opening day and I felt like I was about to appear on television.

In the first inning, I received a scattering of perfunctory applause for making a nice running catch of a routine fly ball that I had initially misjudged. It was hit fairly high, the sun was almost blindingly bright, and for one skittish moment, I had lost it somewhere in the sky. It looked like a falling star, the ball no bigger than a pea. I had started to move backward, a manoeuvre that required me to lunge forward when the ball finally started to come down. I managed to haul it in, the ball safely captured in my glove. It was the final out of the inning. I galloped toward the bench, a few slaps on my back, and looked up into the crowd. My old man was reading a newspaper. He probably hadn't noticed my catch.

At my second time at bat, after hitting a single in my first plate appearance, I walked, not swinging at a crucial pitch that could have I suppose been called strike three. The catcher did not concur with the umpire's verdict and I thought put on a perfectly acceptable display of pique, almost like a major leaguer, kicking up a little dust and then throwing the ball back to the pitcher after saying something unfortunate under his breath to the umpire. He might have called him a stupid ass, a charge that I soon realized would never cause anyone any serious misgiving, particularly when it was made by a twelve year old boy on the edge of a tantrum. In fact, I'm pretty sure that the umpire had laughed. I later completed my heroics during that game by apparently driving in the winning run in the bottom of the seventh inning with my second hit of the game. I specifically remember the first base coach, a man whose name I did not know, suggesting that I had become the game's hero. However, by the time I reached the team bench to accept the congratulations of my teammates, the umpire, a middle aged man who was fat, friendly and made his calls of strikes and balls with a certain theatrical panache, had decided that the run that I had just driven in did not count, the runner on third had allegedly left third base before the pitch that I had hit reached the plate. A peculiar little league rule required base runners to remain on the base until any pitch crossed the plate. The umpire, who received only a mild rebuke from my team manager, a man named Ray who my father told me sold insurance, had judged that my teammate had left third base before the ball that I hit had reached home plate. The run that I had driven in therefore did not count.

As disappointed as I was with having my moment in the spotlight evaporate, my disappointment was transformed into envy when the next batter, a kid named Tessier, managed to drive in the run that I had illegally driven in two or three minutes ago. Tessier, therefore, became the hero and I become a footnote although team manager Ray did pat me on the back for keeping the inning going. Nonetheless, my performance that day did prompt a mention in the sports page of the local weekly, *The Lakeshore News*, the first and maybe the only time that my baseball heroics attracted the attention of the legitimate press. I also remembered that my teammate Pete, who happened to be my best friend at the time, was also cited in the paper, specifically for his defensive play from behind the plate. Almost sixty years later, when I told Pete, who had called me regarding my 69th birthday, that I intended to write about that particular brush with fame when we were both twelve years old, did not offer any disapproval, humorous or otherwise, about including any such trivia in my commentary of our little league experience.

Three games later, an interval during which I tried to perfect my strikeout theatrics on at least two occasions, I was unexpectedly dropped from the team even though I had ostensibly almost driven in the winning run in that first game and picked up hits in the two other games in which I had played. Although I have been known to admit to a number of conflicting stories, I had to admit to myself that I had simply been released because I occasionally played the outfield like a man abandoned on a firing range. I was later told, however, by a former teammate named Burgess, that manager Ray had been convinced that I wasn't serious about my duties as a Valois Yankee when I missed a game because I had to attend, at my father's insistence, a special church event. I sat on the bench until the seventh inning of the next game when manager Ray sent me in to strike out ingloriously against the Cedar Park Cubs. After the game, I was asked to turn in my uniform although I did get to keep the team cap. I may have considered shedding tears. I also considered retirement. Dad may have offered to increase my allowance although I may have just imagined that.

But I was still a player, now relegated to playing first base for a new house league team named McDermott's, which incidentally wore jerseys that were similar in design and colour to the team from which I had recently been dispatched, the Valois Yankees. I had hoped to be assigned to my previous team, Johnson Drug, mainly because I was familiar with the team, having written a composition on my experience with it last fall. But I guess the house league administrators had other ideas and I ended up with a squad sponsored by a local restaurant on Donegani Road, a place which provided counter service, daily dinner specials and large milkshakes that could be had for a quarter. I cannot recall my fortunes or the fortunes of the team that year. In fact, I cannot even remember any of my teammates or the coach. It was obviously an uneventful season. It was 1961. I was twelve years old.

All I can remember from that season were the team colours and the fact I wore number seven, the latter in honour of my hero, Mickey Mantle of the New York Yankees, a baseball player who had become, at least to me and likely millions of kids, not to mention millions of grown men, a mythical figure. He was a monument to an era that is now gone for good, a player that the *Sports Illustrated* magazine called the last great player on the last great team in the last great country. He was the most popular player in the most popular sport during an era when people didn't seem to have a care in the world. I know I didn't. It was also the year that he and his teammate Roger Maris threatened the most cherished record in sports at the time, the 60 home runs that Babe Ruth had hit for the New York Yankees of 1927.

There were hundreds of obituaries written after Mantle passed away on August 13, 1995. It had been almost 30 years since he had last played in a major league game, a tragic figure by then, playing on only one good leg for a New York Yankee team that was no longer respectable, let alone dominant. It had been a sad finale for a player who meant so much for so many for so long. In one of the farewells to the man, even the lordly *Time Magazine* was at pains to eulogize a man who had started playing baseball for the Yankees when Harry Truman was President of the United States and I was two years old.

# INNINGS

There was never any doubt as to his baseball divinity, regardless of the misfortunes that would later become fodder for thousands of press articles. He was simply a hero, my hero, my first hero and maybe, the thought of heroism now receding with age, the only hero I have ever had. Sentimental to be sure, it is absurd to consider the depths to which memory will descend to tranquilize the cynicism of the years since. I would have to plead guilty on all counts. Mickey Charles Mantle was my hero and, in an odd sort of way still was, no true successor having emerged since I first paid tribute to him by insisting on wearing his number seven on my Johnson Drug's jersey in 1960 and most baseball sweaters since. For years, I also coveted and treasured his baseball cards from 1958 on, having once paid over a hundred cards to a kid dumb enough to be willing to trade. That was in 1960.

To me, and many others I imagine, Mantle was born to play baseball, preordained if you will. Everyone intuitively knew that, even those, including Mantle himself, who regarded Mays or Aaron as better players. Everything about him seemed too good to be true. He was too good looking, too much the all American, too much the natural, everything about him too much the characteristic of a great baseball player to be just blind happenstance. Even his name, as the man himself might have pointed out, seemed contrived, as if some advertising flak had come up with the name Mickey Mantle after a few belts at lunch. During the historical season of 1961 when Mantle and Maris pursued the Babe Ruth home run record, a reference to the two of them, no matter how casual, provided sports announcers with too melodious a cadence not to take notice, as if Mel Allen and Red Barber had simply fabricated both names to embellish sports stories that, at least on their face, did not really need the help.

Of course, I knew his life story. His father, a semi-pro ballplayer named Mutt Mantle, who died at the age of 39 years after working his entire life in some Oklahoma mine, had named his son after Detroit Tiger catcher Mickey Cochrane, had taught him to switch hit, something I later took up with dubious results, and had virtually built him into a baseball player of almost unearthly skills. He was so heroic that I devoured all biographical information about him like the fanatic I had become. I was fairly certain that I would have purchased a copy of Footwear Monthly if I knew it contained articles on Mantle's use of sweat socks. Hero worship? Yes, of course. Mania. Maybe. All I pursued, all I wanted as a twelve year old boy was to turn my crystal radio into a divine receiver that, when the stars were right, could have pulled in a game from that Stadium in the Bronx.

Perhaps all such memories are inexplicable melodrama. I was probably too young back then, and likely too naive to be embarrassed about it. I recall the first time I saw Mantle on television, never having had the opportunity to see him in person. Fact was that I had to wait until the Toronto Blue Blue Jays entered the major leagues and by then, Reggie Jackson was the straw that stirred the drink. It was the 1960 season, Detroit the opposition. Mantle, in his second time up, hit one in the second deck of the old Stadium, almost straight in, a line drive, a shot that so impressed announcers Dizzy Dean and Pee Wee Reese, that they sat mute for almost a minute, an event that so unnerved the television audience that they might have thought that something was wrong with their sets. I was transfixed, to have seen, on a black and white set yet, a hero about whom I had read so much time, the occasional newspaper box score as valued as a new Superman comic. I remember Mantle employing that compact almost savage swing to launch a rocket into the stands, no showboat pause in the box to admire it, no bat theatrics, head down to glide around the bases and then into the dugout, as if it were the most pedestrian of events. He was a class act, something natural, something expected, something inevitable.

Yes, I was corny about the whole Mantle thing. Still am I guess. I have had other heroes, other sport luminaries in whom I have taken a particular interest. But they all eventually disappointed me in some way. Not for what they were or became but what they were not or could not be. Brought up in Montreal, I had too many to choose from: the Richards, the Beliveaus, the Cournoyers, the Lafleurs, hockey players all in whom I could have, and usually did, invest considerable interest. But it was not the same somehow, the standard may have been too high. There was Mantle and then there were the others. It was as simple as that.

Mantle was evocative of an era that now seems too good to be true. I have never cared about his personal habits, that he drank like every day would be his last. In fact, he was quoted, before he died, as claiming that "If I knew I was going to live this long, I would have taken better care of myself", a rare burst of irony. I could not have known anything about that anyway. I was twelve years old. In fact, and I supposed he was justified when he expressed revisionist shame toward the end of his life, I was still backward enough to admit that I was terribly impressed when I later read that Mantle had once hit a home run while under the influence. I didn't care whether his status as role model had evaporated with every news story. To me, he was a hero, the best baseball player who ever lived, even though that standing may have declined with age. In 1969, the year after Mantle's retirement, he was third on the list of career home runs, behind only Babe Ruth and Willie Mays. Now he is eighteenth on that list. More than forty years later, the concept of hero now reduced to cynical nostalgia, standing in front of his plaque in the Baseball Hall of Fame in Cooperstown, New York. I was twelve years old again. And that will never go away even though he has.

The whole sports/hero thing for me is summarized in one thought. No matter what happens in the rest of your life, interest in sports is something that cannot be extinguished. President Eisenhower, in reflecting on his own life toward its end, claimed his fondest, if not significant memory was not anything he ever did as President of the United States or even as the commander of the Allied forces in World War II. It was the time he played college football against Red Grange. Even if the story is not true, it should be.

⚾

The remainder of that year with the McDermott's house league team was inauspicious, if not entirely forgettable. To be honest, I would have to admit that I cannot even remember the name of one of my twelve or thirteen teammates. We probably lost more games than we won, as if that mattered to anyone, including our coach, a local man who repaired and sold lawnmowers. His name was Hancock, a large fearsome looking man who apparently was some sort of war hero although, like every other vet in the neighbourhood, there were no known details. As I recall, he constantly smoked Player's Plain cigarettes, so much so that he had developed nice nicotine stains on most of his fingers, one of which was missing, and his upper lip. He also liked to yell a lot, not so much at his players who he seemed to ignore most of the time, but at the umpires who he called idiots. He just like to sit at the head of the team bench, smoking his cigarettes, criticizing the game officials, and enjoy his summer Saturdays. My friend Pete and I were curious enough about Mr. Hancock to visit his repair shop which we were told was located across the train tracks a block up from Lake Saint Louis and the Lakeshore Road. It was a decrepit old garage full of lawnmowers and other machinery. We never saw Coach Hancock. We just stood there in front of his establishment, got scared when we heard the noise of someone hammering something, and ran away, hoping that Mr. Hancock had not seen us trying to spy on him. Not surprisingly, Mr. Hancock did not bother to attend the league banquet where we all ate a chicken dinner on paper plates and watched a bunch of other kids receiving trophies.

The next spring, now too old for little league, having turned thirteen years old the previous January, I passed on an opportunity to try out for the park Pony League team, which was limited to thirteen and fourteen year olds, the middle tier of local youth baseball, Little League below it and Babe Ruth League above it. Unfortunately, the local community association did not provide for house leagues for baseball players above the age of twelve. So I was left that spring with playing baseball in the schoolyard of the Saint John Fisher Elementary School, as it was during previous years. Recess, lunch, after school, you name it. We usually played a game called "Scrub", a variant of baseball played without the convenience of teams. Scores are not kept and the number of players determined the number batting and the number fielding. Usually, twelve to fourteen boys would show up, meaning that four guys would go to bat while the other eight to ten players would play the field. When a batter made an out, he would be banished to right field, the furthest position from the plate. However, if a batted ball was caught in the air, the fielder catching the ball would automatically become the batter. The initial order of the batters was usually determined by whoever was the most intimating of those volunteering to play. They were usually the older guys, the guys who had flunked at least once, if not multiple times. In fact, the most dominating player in those games was a guy named Commander. He was maybe fifteen years old and still dealing with the academic complexities of grade six. My own experience with such games, which I probably pursued every school day between the middle of April and when the school year ended at the end of June, was hardly memorable, at least as far as baseball was concerned. I did, however, occasionally take up switch-hitting, a homage to my hero Mickey Mantle.

Toward the end of that spring, the schoolyard games began later. Many of the players seemed distracted, oddly apathetic. Some, and they were much venerated as a consequence, took to escorting girls to the games and then talking to them throughout the games. Saint John Fisher was a Catholic school with boys attending school in one wing and girls in the other, connected by a common gymnasium and a basement cafeteria. The same gender separation applied to the schoolyard; girls on one side and the boys on the other. The baseball games were sometime delayed because some girl would be standing in the field talking to one of the players. Soon, the games began to migrate toward the girls' side of the schoolyard as more of my classmates took up an interest in conversing with the girls rather than playing baseball. Not only were the games delayed but they were often stopped entirely. Understandably, I too began to drift over to the other side of the yard, there being little other choice. For me and several of my less cosmopolitan colleagues, this consisted mainly of standing on the edge of the crowd and staring at the girls, occasionally throwing a baseball around but showing little practical interest in actually playing baseball.

For me, and perhaps a few others, even a few days of this were enough to ruin the game. We were sharing the field with a crowd of twelve and thirteen year girls; all giggles and misapplied lipstick, Catholic school tunics and knee socks, and mysteries about which I would spend much of the rest of my life investigating. I made several brave, or as brave as I could be at thirteen years old, attempts at conversations. I made little headway. In return for my efforts, efforts which I made with considerable psychological preparation, I received no relief from my fears. Instead, I was provided with a virtual thesaurus of dismissive responses: snickers, giggles, smirks, titters, even the occasional chuckle would come my way. I hardly spoke to any of the girls. If the wind was right, you could hear the girls trading confidences with each other. Or I thought. I would pretend to be indifferent even though I was usually interested in the most mundane remark I could hear, particularly if I thought they were being directed to me.

That summer, my last summer before I was faced with the anxieties of high school, I played little baseball, having no team to play for, no league to play in. I usually spent most of my weekday mornings hanging around at the park, joining the occasional pick up game. I would throw the ball around with whoever showed up, my glove always with me. Sometimes, someone would bring a bat and we would hit fly balls and grounders to each other, basically forcing ourselves to practice for a team that did not exist. In the afternoon, we went swimming at the community pool. Then, on the weekends, we attended the occasional Pony League game. The more of those games I saw, the more I regretted not trying out for the local Pony League team. In fact, I would not play or even try out for another organized baseball team for almost a decade, my athletic activities limited to football, hockey and a panoply of high school and college house league sports which, strangely enough, did not include baseball.

# THE BALL SEEMS FASTER

**A**s mentioned, from the early 1960s on, I did not play an inning of organized baseball for almost ten years, the exception being intramural high school softball although the two teams on which I played really didn't seem to know how to actually play the game. I cannot recall my reasoning for not pursuing baseball. Either there was no local team for which to play or I was no longer interested in finding one. Aside from softball, I did play for a number of sports for other teams, at least a number of other high school teams. I played for three high school varsity teams, two football and one hockey, four house league teams in hockey and football, and countless intramural class teams, including a number playing relatively obscure sports like billiards, bowling, swimming and tennis. I did play a couple of softball games, admittedly a close variant of baseball, the obvious distinction being the size of the ball. My experiences with the class softball teams were, however, hardly memorable. Fact was that there were only five or six guys on the team, myself included, who seemed to be even remotely familiar with baseball or softball. In any event, we played softball for only two of the four years I was in high school, the other two years not offering softball as a class sport. In addition, the games, the results of which I cannot recall, were limited to a tournament format: lose one game and the team is out. No wonder I cannot remember playing any of the games. There may have been only two of them.

Over my five years of college, I did not play any baseball or any variant of baseball. While there were doubtless baseball leagues on the entire island of Montreal in which I could have played if I had made the effort, I did not bother. I have no explanation aside from assumed indifference. I did play intramural touch football and hockey but that was about it, fewer opportunities for athletics in college than high school, or at least fewer opportunities where I went, specifically Loyola College in Montreal. The only baseball I did play during those years took place on Saturdays or Sundays or both in the local park where I had played Little League maybe five or six years before. On those days, I would haul myself, my bat, a well chipped Adirondack, my glove, a battered Rawlings model that I had acquired from a kid who apparently was no longer interested in playing, and half a dozen profoundly used baseballs, all of which were appropriately scuffed, loose stitching and almost falling apart. It was basically a return to those haphazard games of "Scrub" that I had played in schoolyards past.

I would convince my youngest brother, sometimes threateningly, to accompany me, my ultimate purpose to provide me with a two man batting practice or at least someone with whom to play catch. But sometimes, I was fortunate enough to find other guys looking for a game. We would play abbreviated "Scrub" or if there were enough players, somehow dividing the group into two teams and actually playing a game, sometimes keeping score, sometimes not keeping score. Unfortunately, the same guys did not show up every day, actual games therefore were not a regular occurrence, two Saturdays a month the norm I guess. Sometimes, only several times over the entire summer, only my brother John and I would be available. We would practice for a hour or so, that is if John agreed to stay around for more than fifteen minutes or so, his reluctance kind of ironic considering that within little more than a decade he was founding a baseball league in Ottawa, a league that started with six teams in 1982 and now features thirty seven teams. John passed away several years ago, his baseball playing days more than twenty five years in the past but his baseball legacy secure nevertheless. He was never a particularly good player, his athletic gifts barely evident. Fact was that he was barely serviceable as a player although he compensated for his limitations as an athlete with his exuberance, which sometimes seemed almost embarrassing, if not unnatural.

In any event, my brother and I pursued those pickup games in the park for two or three summers, my only connection to baseball now as informal and casual as those backyard wiffle ball games we used to play. I never got the opportunity to play on any legitimate team in those years. One of my co-workers in a chainsaw manufacturing plant, where I had secured summer employment for three successive years and for which I received a cool $1.66 an hour for performing dangerous assembly line work, claimed to be trying out for a junior baseball team in Dorval, a nearby suburb. My interest dissipated, if not disappeared, however, when he told me that more than a hundred eighteen and nineteen year old hopefuls were trying out for the team and that most of them, including the maybe eighty guys who would eventually be cut from the team, had experience playing in lower tier leagues, the Babe Ruth and Pony leagues being the most prominent. Since I had not played any organized baseball for maybe six or seven years, my stint with the McDermott's team unlikely to be highly regarded, I concluded that I was not qualified for such a team.

Accordingly, I courageously declined to even consider auditioning for the Dorval team, the embarrassment of being released after one practice as inevitable as swinging unsuccessfully at a Sandy Koufax fastball. My co-worker later told me that I had been wise not to waste my time, his determination being that the team manager, who supposedly had played professionally in the minors, had high standards.

I finally graduated from Loyola College in the spring of 1971 and then moved to Ottawa that fall to attend journalism school, a ridiculous waste of time in hindsight. Aside from the occasional mixed touch football game with my new university colleagues, one of whom I eventually moved in with, I did not play any sports. It was not until the next spring, after I had to drop out of the Carleton University journalism school for financial reasons, that baseball was re-introduced to me. With a future that began to look increasingly bleak, at least from the view of perspective of employment, for which I was pretty well desperate, I started as a general labourer for the Royal Canadian Mint, where I was paid $4.00 an hour, a virtual fortune compared to the wages I was earning from the part time janitor's job I was compelled to procure that winter when I ran out of money. I started at the Mint in June of 1972. I was assigned to the examining room where I sat in front of a conveyor belt staring hypnotically at freshly minted pennies, nickels, dimes, and quarters, looking for flaws.

Within a week, I was invited by a fellow examining room worker to join the Mint fastball team, a sport about which I feigned more familiarity than I actually had. According to Norm, the team manager to whom I was introduced in the plant locker room, there were several open spots on the roster. When I explained that my fastball experience was basically limited to casual slow pitch softball games and little league baseball, Norm shrugged, suggesting that there were few differences between the two sports, aside of course from the size of the ball, the distance between the bases, and most importantly, the distance between the pitcher's rubber and the plate. That is when I realized that baseball and softball were two things but fastball was another.

In our first game, we were scheduled to play against a team sponsored by a local car dealership. Apparently, the league in which the Mint played also included teams that did not represent any government department or agency. I was told that there were eighteen teams in the league, a third of which were from outside government, several car dealerships, a restaurant, an insurance company, and two sports clubs, teams from Ottawa and teams from across the Ottawa River in Hull.

With my debut game due within three days, I had brought my glove to work, the same Rawlings mitt that I had been using since I played little league. I managed to convince another guy from the examining room, who was already playing for several of the plant teams, including the fastball team, to throw the ball around with me, out in the back of the plant. He told me to buy a new glove, preferably a used glove. It was obvious, at least to me, that my old baseball glove was not ample enough to confidently catch the much larger softball. The next day, I purchased a used softball glove, this one by Spalding, at a local used sports equipment store, a couple of blocks from my $85 a month apartment, that bachelor pad that comfortably housed my girlfriend, still a student and to whom I was engaged to marry at the end of the summer, and myself. It did not take me long to get accustomed to handling the softball. It was curious. By the time, our second pitch and catch session was over, I seemed to be more competent fielding the softball than my new teammate from the examining room, a guy named Gordie, who I was told was a much more talented hockey player.

I arrived well in advance of the game, which was to be played at one of the four softball diamonds on Riverside Drive. I did not realize how significant the differences between baseball, softball and fastball were until I arrived forty five minutes before the game and saw our pitcher, a rather large man named Murray, throwing a softball in a windmill motion as fast as a baseball from a pitching rubber. The difference was that the pitching rubber was fifteen feet closer to the plate than it was in baseball. I also noticed that Murray would leap toward the plate as he released the ball, making the distance between the pitcher and the plate appear to be even closer. I stood behind the plate protected by the backstop, and instantly identified the rationale for all the bunting that was recommended for fastball games. I also concluded that there must be a lot of strikeouts in fastball and wondered about the catcher who had to handle that pitching. His fielding responsibilities would be more like that of a hockey goalie, albeit without the same equipment. Playing behind the plate for the Mint team was a guy named Gilles.

I was admittedly nervous, not having playing any kind of proper ball game since I was thirteen years old. Norm, everybody called him Big Norm, handed me a white sweater with "MINT" emblazoned in red across the front of a blue sweater and the requested number "7" on the back. He informed me that I would be playing third base, advising me to always look for the bunt, and then instructed me to take a little infield practice. Big Norm started to hit us grounders. Aside from myself, there were guys named Dave at first, Ed at second, and Roy at shortstop. Big Norm told me to play well in front of the third base bag, explaining that the bunt down the third base line was the most frequent play for right handed hitters in fastball. While the throw to first was less of an effort than if I was playing even or behind the third base bag, I was a little concerned if the opposition hitters decided not to bunt. I shared my anxiety with Gordie, who played in right field, who confided that pretty well anyone who played third base in fastball made the same observation and expressed the same concern. Gordie admitted that he had been fortunate in being handed the right field assignment for the game, suggesting that, with big Murray pitching, it was unlikely that anyone would actually hit a ball in his direction, the potential for an embarrassing fielding error fairly low.

I remember that game in particular because it was the first time I had ever faced a fastball pitcher. I went to the plate three times that evening, batting ninth which seemed entirely appropriate given that it was my first fastball game, and returned to the bench after taking unsuccessful swings at nine pitches that seemed to be screaming toward the plate, travelling much faster than any I had ever seen anywhere except perhaps at the Expo games I used to attend when I still lived in Montreal. In addition, on top of the speed of the pitches, the pitcher for the Turpin Pontiac team, who was a trifle slimmer than Murray but still relatively rotund, seemed to be ten feet away from me when he released the ball. As a result, my first time up, I had to concentrate on not ducking out of the way of the pitch. My gymnastics did not, however, prevent me from swinging at every pitch and missing, sometimes by a foot or more. Not that every motion of my bat was an actual swing. Further to Big Norm's exhortations, of the nine balls at which I actually swung, five were attempted bunts, pathetic swipes at pitches that I could barely see. In addition, in the process of another one of my unsuccessful attempts at hitting one of those pitches, I lost control of the bat, it almost flying over the backstop, the predictable outcome of a change up thrown by the Turpin pitcher.

In the end, we won that game 2-1, the result of a single hit, a ball hit to the right field fence hit by supposedly our best hitter, a lift truck driver named Ron, two walks and an error by their second baseman. For his part, our pitcher Murray gave up two hits, one of which I did field but didn't have the time to make the throw to first. Murray struck out eighteen in seven innings, the other three outs were two easy popups to the infield and a dribbler to the pitcher. At the next opportunity, the following day at work, after summoning the courage to actually approach Ron, his prolific lift truck driving having provided him with an intimidating reputation, I asked him how he managed to hit his double and a pair of impressive fly outs while the rest of the lineup couldn't hit a ball out of the infield. After snickering and feigning a blow to my shoulder, he told me that he usually started to swing either as or just before the pitcher released the ball. I didn't know whether Ron the lift truck driver was serious. It took me a couple more games of offensive futility to realize that he was.

During those next few games, the results of which I cannot recall, I tested several different batting stances, bat held high, bat held low, chocking up, feet together, feet apart, front foot in the bucket, feet in warrior pose, foretelling the yoga my wife and I would take up forty years later, trying to copy the batting postures of various major leaguers, even going back to batting right handed, my original choice before I started impersonating my hero, Mickey Mantle, by batting left handed. Following the advice of lift truck driver Ron, I began to achieve some sort of success in hitting fastballs when I began to start my swing just as the pitcher was releasing the ball. Some of the time though, quite a lot of the time actually,

# INNINGS

I would end up looking foolish as I did before I started experimenting with the Ron method of hitting, sometimes missing the ball by a foot or more, prompting little more than sympathetic nods from teammates who were more often than not looking forward to the same fate. The explanation was simple enough. In addition to speed, fastball pitchers used risers, drop balls, curves, and change ups to fool presumably befuddled hitters, myself among them.

Still, despite my frequent failures, I began to successfully execute the occasional bunt. By the fifth or sixth game, I started to successfully hit balls out of the infield, some of which began to land safely. Most, if not all of my so-called hits, my most significant of which was a double I hit down the third base line, were struck to the opposite field. Simply put, I was never able to pull the ball, which supposedly indicated that I could not generate enough bat speed to meet the ball before it got past my primary hitting zone, i.e. before the ball travelled past my front foot, or I was told. I will admit that I have long ruminated about the mystery of my inability to pull the ball. In fact, almost fifty years later, playing slow pitch, the direction of my hits are so predictable that most opponents started to apply a defensive shift on me almost every time I came to the plate, a strategy that would have been unheard years before. In any event and to my constant disappointment, it worked most of the time. I would occasionally visit local batting cages to refine my stroke, to somehow educate myself to hit the ball toward right rather than left field, the latter being the expected path of most of my batted balls, regardless of whether they landed safely or resulted in just another mundane out. Unfortunately, my education proved lacking, right to the end.

I played fastball with the team representing the Royal Canadian Mint for only one more season, because of my untimely decision to leave the place, which was mainly due to the recent resignation of a good friend and the fact that I had grown weary of continually dodging the foreman regarding my shortcomings, i.e. unacceptably long hair and not wearing the appropriate safety gear on the plant floor. It is curious. Almost forty five years later and I can still remember most of my teammates on that team. It is really not that surprising that my recollections are that faithful. Most of the guys on the fastball team also played hockey. Since the hockey team was much more important to the plant staff than the fastball team, if you played on both teams, you were memorable. In fact, the Mint hockey team was often afforded certain privileges, like leaving shifts early on game days, coming in late the day after a game, and even getting the occasional day off during playoffs. The fastball team did not enjoy such privileges nor did the touch football team, another Mint enterprise for which I played.

The Mint was a small operation compared to say the Post Office, Revenue Canada or Health Canada and therefore had many fewer potential players to draw on for their teams. Still, we probably won more games than we lost, which was remarkable considering the number of players on which we could draw. For example, I do recall that when I tendered my resignation from the Mint. Big Norm, who managed the fastball team as well as coaching the hockey team, told me that he was sad to see me go, grumbling about the trouble he was going to face replacing me on both the baseball and hockey teams. Leaving those teams was the only regret I ever had about resigning from the Mint although I would occasionally reconsider my regret when I thought about my career prospects if I had stayed. In that regard, years later, I was informed by somebody who still worked there that senior management of the place was now populated by guys who quite frankly I thought were not executive material. Besides, had I stayed on rather than quit so prematurely, my retirement date would have been earlier and my retirement likely more affluent.

Funny thing. While I eventually found employment in another government department, specifically the Department of Industry, Trade and Commerce and subsequently replaced and renamed Department of Foreign Affairs and International Trade, I never played another game for any sort for a government department or agency. I have no explanation.

# ORIGINS OF A BASEBALL LEAGUE

It was a few years later. I had moved several times, managed to work a number pointless jobs without staying in any of them longer than six months, and casually accepted a divorce initiated by a first wife, someone I would never really see again. It might have been 1976 or 1977 when my youngest brother John, the same youngest brother who I persuaded and sometimes compelled to join me in those pick up baseball games in Valois Park, moved into my one bedroom apartment on Frank Street, just east of Bank Street in downtown Ottawa. While I had undertaken my usual temporary stint at the tax department, pulling down a cool $4.50 an hour as a clerk, John was fashioning himself a career in the retail sector, working in the basement of the Hudson's Bay store on Rideau Street, a fitting ambition for a man with a Bachelor of Arts with a major in Russian history. He worked in the boys' department, selling jeans, t-shirts, underwear, socks and other juvenile paraphernalia to mothers who invariably looked like they wanted to be somewhere else. As far as I knew, John was an exceedingly enterprising salesman, invariably attracting the attention of management, so I was told by one of his co-workers. Within maybe two months, both of us had come to the conclusion that we needed a larger apartment, that is if we wanted to continue sharing accommodation. Accordingly, John was able to lease a two bedroom apartment in an older building called the Ambassador Court. It was a couple of blocks south on Bank Street.

Around the time we moved into the Ambassador Court, John told me that one of his associates from the Hudson's Bay played a pick up game every Sunday morning at one of the two baseball diamonds over by the Ottawa General Hospital on Smyth Road. They were called Lynda Lane and Potter Field. Although I cannot recall with any historical certainty,

I think they played on the smaller diamond, the one called Lynda Lane. Both were fenced in but neither were equipped with lights for evening play. Lynda Lane had a grass infield while the infield on Potter was gravel. Apparently, as I was later to discover, two organizations turned out to hold exclusive permits for use of the diamonds, the local Senior Interprovincial Baseball League for Potter and the Alta Vista Little League for Lynda Lane. However, at least according to John's friend from the Hudson's Bay, no one played there on Sunday mornings. That's when the pickup games were played. Sometime in the summer of 1977, John was invited to join the Sunday morning games. He asked me to join him. Luckily, we both had baseball gloves although I cannot recall John ever playing on a baseball team of any kind.

The Sunday morning games were organized by Bruce Harvey, a local guy who was working at the Bay with John. He had a lot of friends, both from high school, the precise location of which I never knew, and the University of Ottawa. He must have convinced most of them to show up on Sunday mornings. There was almost always enough players to field two teams, one of which was usually comprised of Bruce and his high school friends, many of whom I can actually remember after forty years or so. Admittedly, however, a number of them were to eventually play in the Ottawa Recreation Baseball League, the organization that eventually grew out of these pick up games. There were three brothers named Mackey, two brothers named Dean, two guys named O'Connor who were not brothers, a tall red haired slugger who everybody called called JK, and three other guys. They were named Al, Blair, and Dave. In addition, there were a number of University of Ottawa students, some of whom had played on the university football team and were therefore acceptably athletic, particularly for a Sunday morning sandlot baseball game.

John and I were always assigned to the team that opposed the team headed by Bruce and his friends. The names of the guys on our team, the opposition team, were forgettable for the most part. Over the next three years, the Sunday morning games continued pretty well unabated, albeit with different rosters each game. Several of my own friends as well as a few co-workers in the Department of Industry, Trade and Commerce, which I had joined for good toward the end of 1977, were persuaded to join the games. Several years later, employing something resembling total recall, I was able to reconstruct a gallery of guys who had come and gone during the three years we played those pick up games. Maybe it was my imagination but I eventually calculated that up to fifty guys had actually showed up for at least one of those games. In fact, some Sundays, there were maybe fifteen players on each side, an intolerable situation particularly for the guys who showed up most if not all of the time. Understandably, the next Sundays were not so well populated.

Aside from the lack of predictability regarding the number of players on each Sunday, there was the problem of city permits to play on the Lynda Lane diamond. It seemed that every month or so during those years and several successive years as well, the police would show up to order us off the diamond, claiming that one of the local little leagues had a permit for the exclusive use of the diamond. When we questioned the viability of such a permit, a copy of which was never shown to any of us at any time, the police would invariably become stern, if not hostile. They would refer us to city hall or the president of the little league that was claiming jurisdiction over the diamond. We would point out, cleverly we thought, that it was unlikely, if not impossible that any little league would need a permit to use any baseball diamond seven days a week, twenty four hours a day. The police would usually shrug, some would smirk, and then demand that we depart immediately. They would actually wait until we left, usually for the closest field, a small diamond behind a school on the other side of Smyth Road, never going near Potter, the adjoining field for which the Senior International Baseball League held the permit. The school diamond posed another kind of problem. Backyards of local houses in the relatively upscale neighbourhood of Alta Vista circled the field. In view of the smaller size of the field, otherwise modest fly balls could find their way over the fence and into the backwards. When that happened, local homeowners would often threaten dire consequences, usually using predictable invective. These episodes would sometimes result in visits from the police, sometimes they didn't.

Not surprisingly, the relative abilities of the players who showed up for the games in those days were understandably varied. There were a number of guys, my brother being one of them, who appeared to be more or less just learning the game although their incompetence was more the effect of a lack of athletic ability than it was based on ignorance about the game.

Some of them were spectacular enough in their ineptitude as to be quite memorable. There was a guy named Gerry who arrived at Lynda Lane one Sunday, uninvited most of us assumed, wearing two brand new batting gloves on his left hand, a fielding glove that was so stiff that one would be better off using one of those oven mitts that old timers used, and carrying a baseball bat that looked like it had been produced on a lathe. The bat had supposedly been made of wood but felt like it was made of lead. In that context, we were almost always burdened with wooden bats in those days, the expense of aluminum bats delaying their use until maybe four or five years later, by which time the Ottawa Recreational Baseball League had been established. On top of the equipment shortcomings, poor Gerry also violated several fashion standards, the most significant of which was a bucket hat and a striped golf shirt. As a final disability, Gerry was a terrible baseball player, even if one could actually apply the term player to him.

There was also a guy named who appeared to be afflicted with some sort of disability, a handicap that limited practically everything he did on a baseball field. In fact, he actually thought he was a player but did not seem to be familiar with its basic rules. Other particularly memorable members of the baseball inept included a chubby kid that wore flannel trousers, a white shirt and necktie and often seemed to be in a hypnotic state, a nervous looking kid who always struck out and couldn't catch a ball unless you placed it into his glove and several long hairs who seemed to be and likely were high most of the time.

Then there was my brother John himself, who insisted on catching for some reason, his short tenure as a goalie on an atom house league hockey team a decade or so past the likely basis for the choice. Although John's catching was acceptable, a superior throwing arm more than compensation for a weak glove, he couldn't hit worth a damn, even when given every opportunity. He was also slow, sometimes running out of breath trying to make it to first base. While John ran the bases, as one sage commentator was to observe, he looked like he was carrying two suitcases. Since it was obvious that John was hardly alone in his limitations as a player, they were generally disregarded, particularly in view of the fact that John was unusually enthusiastic about a game that had generally eluded him. He even joined the other players in criticizing and making light of the foibles of those who demonstrated that they were deficient in some area of the game, whether it was at the plate or in the field. Fact was that one of the more attractive aspects of those Sunday morning gatherings was the opportunities for mirth that some of the more laughable examples of baseball absurdities that those games provided.

There were predictable prescriptions about playing a game that was so casual in origin. The rules, although roughly based on normal baseball standards, were flexible enough to permit a number of deviations. First of all, the normal consideration of balls and strikes did not apply. Basically, and not to suggest that there were never any exceptions, hitters were permitted to stand at the plate until they hit a ball into fair territory or went down on strikes. There were no walks and no called strikes. At times, quite a few times actually, particularly selective batters, some of whom might have been either blind, neurotic, or existentially patient about their own prowess, would stand at the plate watching twenty or thirty pitches sail by without swinging at any of them.

Strangely enough, this kind of absurdly discriminating approach to hitting would inevitably lead to the formation of a three, four and then six team league. John, the future founder and first commissioner of what would later become known as the Ottawa Recreational Baseball League, often recalled, with a certain ironic delight, that he could ascribe the formation of that enterprise to one particular guy who often took an extremely inordinate time at the plate during those pickup years, looking over every pitch from increasingly exhausted pitchers like he was examining the Death Sea Scrolls. The complaints from other players sometimes threatened to capsize the Sunday morning games themselves.

Not that every player who went to the plate took their time but enough did to contribute to a game speed that was profoundly sluggish. Looking back, compared to the current criticism that the interval between pitches in the major leagues has increased by about two seconds over the past few seasons, the pace of the games that we used to play on those Sunday mornings at Lynda Lane was positively glacial, so slow that players began to turn to a variety of diversions. Many smoked, this was after all the late 1970s, dragging on cigarettes as they continued to hope that whoever was presiding at the plate was there to swing the bat at pitches rather than watching them. Some took to drinking, casually swigging on canned beer or metal flasks or even Coke bottles. Others were even reclining in the field, completely apathetic to the so-called game going on around them. It seemed that the only participants that were actually engaged were the pitchers, many of whom were on the edge of nervous breakdowns, the occasionally disinterested batters and the catchers, many of whom were so weary that they were dropping every second pitch and were having trouble throwing the ball back to the pitcher. Ennui was widespread. Two of these catchers actually resigned from their positions during the actual games, so frustrated were they with games that seemed more like chess than baseball. While nobody saw one of the erstwhile catchers again, no one remembering his name, the other returned to play the next week, the prodigal predictably insisting that he never play behind the plate again.

Then there was the continual stream of expletives, the discomfort of standing around in the field waiting for someone to actually hit a ball to them prompting an unfortunate expulsion of curses, some more determined than others to bully indolent batters into swinging at pitches that they might otherwise pass up. In addition, teammates joined their opponents in swearing at batters who were taking their time selecting a pitch to swing at. While a few of these recalcitrant batters actually took notice of the avalanche of criticism, most did not, shrugging off the profanity by simply ignoring it. Some even took pleasure in the disregard of criticism, including one guy who laughed at the expletives like they were witticisms at a cocktail party. It reminded me of a boy named Ian with whom I had played pee wee hockey back in Valois. Ian, whose abilities as a hockey player were modest to say the least, at times used to take delight in scoring on his own net. In any event, the pace at which these games were played become one of their memorable aspects and doubtlessly contributed to the establishment of more organized games.

Notwithstanding some of the less laudatory aspects of those Sunday morning games, which admittedly did provide a fair bit of entertainment for all, they did feature a number of skilled baseball players. Many of the original game organizer Bruce Harvey's friends were competent enough, so much so that most of them would eventually form one of the founding teams of the Ottawa Recreational Baseball League in 1982, first called Stony Mondays before finally settling on Sun Devils. I specifically remember a number of them: a couple of outfielders who occasionally managed to hit balls over the fence at Lynda Lane, including one who invariably forced outfielders to play him on the warning track; a catcher who not only could hit but was a proficient defensive player; a couple of pitchers who could but often did not throw hard for fear of scaring skittish batters; the three MacKay brothers; and several University of Ottawa varsity football players. As far as I was concerned, I guess I could say that I wasn't a standout player but I may have been better than most.

After three years of casual sandlot games on Sunday mornings, a decision was made to formalize them by forming a genuine baseball league with three teams, a schedule, and umpiring of sorts, each team calling its own balls and strikes. It was less a decision, however, than an evolution, a conclusion reached mainly by my brother John who most certainly shared the general discontent regarding the way the games were being played. I cannot recall who actually first suggested the idea but it was definitely John who convinced enough of the Sunday morning players to agree to what seemed to be somewhat of an eccentric idea at the time. He eventually attracted enough interest to form three teams to play a rudimentary schedule, each team to play doubleheaders every second Sunday to ensure that each team would eventually play the same number of games, the concept of games during the weekday evenings yet to be considered.

As best as I can recollect, my brother having passed away and therefore not around to verify any of my historical recollections, the three teams were: the aforementioned Stony Mondays, comprised pretty well entirely of Bruce Harvey and his friends, an incidental irony being that Bruce Harvey, who was a fairly decent player himself, did not play beyond that first year; Central Mortgage and Housing, a group of government guys who I had invited to the Sunday morning games; and the Blacks, our team, the usual assortment of guys, friends and friends of friends. As for the strange team name, I cannot attest to its origin, any alternatives equally forgettable, unable to remember even one of them. Although it cannot be unmistakably confirmed, the team biography, which was first recorded in 1983 with the appearance of *Baseball Ottawa*, a pretentiously though simply titled journal that the Blacks and then its successor team the Dukes published for more than 25 years, recorded the first game taking place sometime in June 1980.

That inaugural season, which was played without any statistical account whatever being kept, ended prematurely when the Central Mortgage and Housing team forfeited several games in succession, effectively disbanding the league, at least for the remainder of that year. Amazingly enough, the more formalized structure of an actual league proved relatively free of difficulty except for the inconclusive end of that first season. We scheduled games, we kept score, we tabulated standings, and most importantly, we were actually able to officiate the games by ourselves without memorable incident. Sure, with catchers calling balls and strikes, not to mention the bases, there were bound to be disagreements, particularly when the catchers making the determinations had a tentative grasp of the strike zone. Although there were only three teams in the league, there were probably six or seven players who actually played the position that season and therefore were charged with umpiring. Yes, there were a multitude of obvious mistakes; balls bouncing in front of the plate or a foot outside being called strikes, pitches thrown down the middle called balls, walks granted on three balls, counts forgotten, foul balls misjudged, rules on infield flies and balks misinterpreted, all of which were handled with a dismissive laugh or a frustrated shrug. To be honest, I cannot recall nor was I informed of any serious dispute erupting over any specific umpiring decision. It was generally agreed, however, that employing legitimate officials would probably be preferable than having catchers masquerade as umpires.

While we managed to play most of those games at Lynda Lane, if not one or two at Potter, the adjacent diamond on Smyth Road, we were occasionally forced to move the games to an apparently abandoned facility off Walkley Road, near the Airport Parkway. It was called Linton Park, a large fenced field that had been situated in the middle of another suburban housing development, just like the diamond behind the Samuel Genest school on Smyth. Like the reaction to our games at that diamond, our games there were not welcomed by the neighbourhood. The only access to the field from a surrounding suburban street was an asphalt path cut between two houses. Any game at the field invariably resulted in a throng of parked cars on the street, something that was not normally seen on that street at any time, day or night. There were complaints, precipitated not only by the parked cars but more particularly by the boisterous behaviour produced by maybe two dozen ball players involved in post-game festivities. The police would be notified, they would arrive, we would hurriedly hide the beers we had been drinking, they would inform us of the neighbourhood objections, and then would issue us with warnings about drinking in public and illegal parking, the latter a strange admonition since none of our cars were parked illegally, only inconveniently. The police— there were usually two officers, one of whom looked slightly embarrassed — would also ask whether we had a permit to use the field, a familiar inquiry that we would always answer in the negative. Applications for a city permit to use any of the baseball diamonds we had used in the previous few years had been ritualistically denied by the City of Ottawa, no reasons provided. At the time of the Linton Park incidents, my brother, who was the individual who had been applying for the permits, said that he intended to appear before the city council in a baseball uniform if that's what it took. He said that he intended to do so in the spring, before the next baseball season.

John made good on his promise before the 1981 season when the league he had founded the previous year was reformed with four teams. Stony Monday's and the Blacks reappeared for a second year while two new outfits, the mysteriously named the DH and DL, joined. The former team, the strangely named DH was based mainly on remnants of the disbanded Central Mortgage and Housing team while the latter, the so-called DL, was formed after John met some guys already playing pickup baseball in a diamond off Preston Street, a neighbourhood into which John himself had moved the previous year. The next year, they would be rechristened the Sweat Sox, a name that they still retain today. Stony Monday's roster appeared to be identical to the previous year while our team, the Blacks, were augmented by a couple of guys after John advertised for players in the personal section of the *Ottawa Citizen*.

As far as I can recall, there were a number of differences between the 1981 season and the previous year, all improvements one could argue. The even number of teams made it easier to construct a schedule, arrangements were made for an umpire to officiate each game, a fee of maybe $30 or so was charged, a couple of bucks collected from each player before the game was the procedure, and John was finally able to obtain a permit to play at Lynda Lane, an achievement that did require his appearance at city council. He did not report as to whether he had appeared at the council meeting in a baseball uniform. But John did report that the only opposition to his application was from the head of a local little league association, a man who John recognized as having invited the cops to Lynda Lane to complain about our playing there several years ago. At the council meeting, the man, who John suggested looked like Elmer Fudd with a moustache, protested that we were setting a bad example for the little leaguers, frequent profanity, cigarette smoking during the games, no umpires and an absence of uniforms being cited as his primary objections. When council did grant John a permit, they actually apologized to Mr. Fudd, an indication John said of the man's inexplicable political influence.

The 1981 season was entirely forgettable, specific details unrecorded, at least by me. The DH team folded, dropping out of the league in August of that summer, apparently because half of the squad found themselves on vacation during the same three week period, a circumstance that led to a half a dozen games being cancelled. John admitted, as de facto commissioner of the league, that he would have thrown DH out of the league if it had not folded first, for the inconvenience alone. John also said that DH was a difficult team to handle anyway, no surprise for a group of government bureaucrats. That season ended with the Blacks winning the first league championship after it supposedly snowed in early October. The Blacks won because they had already won its only two games in the round robin championship series.

During the fall and winter that followed that season, John and I discussed the possibility of formalizing the league even further, adding three more teams, interest generated by guys contacting John in response to the ads he had placed in newspaper personals, arranging for two umpires for each game, insisting that each team wear uniforms, and officially naming the newly established league the Ottawa Recreational Baseball League (ORBL). In March 1982, representatives of six teams, the three surviving from the previous year, and three new teams, namely the Astros, the Red Eyes, a team put together by two or three of the former members of the disbanded DH, and the Swingers, another team with a lot of guys with Italian names who lived in the Preston Street area. In addition, Stoney Mondays changed its name to Sun Devils, which was generally thought to be a football team moniker, while the Blacks were still called the Blacks although they would change it to the Dukes of Somerset the next year, the latter reflecting the sponsorship of a bar on Somerset Street where John often lunched. Ironically, the Dukes were associated with a bar that for the next two years thought it was sponsoring a team that played soccer.

On that point, the Dukes never visited its sponsor for at least two years, it being located downtown on Somerset Street, well away from the Lynda Lane diamond, where they played their games. Two years later, sometime during the summer of 1984, they actually dropped by the Duke of Somerset for post-game beers, the sudden motive forgotten, at least by me. The bar manager, an expatriate Irishman named Sam McFall, noticed that their uniforms hardly looked like they belonged on guys playing soccer. As I recall, most of the other patrons in the Duke of Somerset that night agreed with Mr. McFall's assessment. I think we never got past our first pint, the brand selection a little exotic for us anyway, before we departed, our embarrassment as obvious as that of Mr. McFall. Although we continue to retain the name Dukes, it having survived until this present day, we dropped any reference to Somerset, the bar having terminated its sponsorship after having us there that night. According to John, at least he apologized for the misunderstanding.

During that first year, like the next two or three years, the actual playing of baseball was entirely forgettable, fairly ragged, no way to measure. We began the 1982 season by travelling to Montreal where a few players from each of three ORBL teams, an all star team if you will, losing 6-1 to a team representing the Montreal Recreational Baseball League. I can't remember who had organized the game. As far as I can recall, a catcher named Larry Johnson, who would go on to play for the Blacks and then the Dukes for five years, a guy named Barry who played pick up with us for several years but never played another game for us after that game in Montreal, and John and I represented the Blacks/Dukes.

Strangely enough, although I am certain that the Black/Duke roster had more players, I could only find statistics for nine players for the 1982 season. There was a guy named Ben Cornick, who may have gone on to a career in politics and/or public service after gracing the Blacks/Dukes for the next two years, he having constantly spoken about those possibilities. While Cornick was not much of a hitter, he was the only one player who accomplished the famed Cesar Tovar/Bert Campaneris feat of playing every fielding position in one game. In the case of the Blacks/Dukes, however, the feat was considered in the context of one season rather than one game. The only other Black/Duke to accomplish the exploit was yours truly. I should emphasize, however, that over the 26 seasons I spent with the Blacks/Dukes, several dozens of my teammates could have easily duplicated it if given the opportunity. After Mr. Cornick, there was our regular catcher during those early years, Larry Johnson, whose personality quirks and peculiar expressions often overshadowed the fact that he was a decent catcher and a good hitter with speed and a penchant for stolen bases. Following Johnson was soft spoken and smooth hitting outfield Gary Lindfield, who joined the team after stopping by the field one day and simply asking to play. There was Jack Livingstone, an accountant who was one of the team's regular pitchers and its regular shortstop when he wasn't pitching. The ace of the pitching staff was the soft spoken Rob Power who won four of the five games the team won over the entire 1982 season, striking out 59 batters in the 46 innings he pitched. Rob would leave the team the next year only to return the year after that. A work colleague of mine, a former junior hockey player named Paul Yakabuski, rounded out the pitching rotation although with limited success. At second base was another quiet performer, a man named Scott McDonald who had a bum leg and an inability to hit above the unfortunate Mendonza line batting average of .200. Also in the outfield was Steve Williams, attracted to the team by one of John's newspaper advertisements. He was a player barely out of his teens who first used to show up at the games attired in corduroy trousers and other examples of Big Steel Man fashion sense. He possessed an exemplary throwing arm and was fated in the future to become a player of some repute. Then there was John and I, he spelling Johnson behind the plate and me playing first base and leading the team in hitting.

There were a number of other guys, now forgotten, who filled in when the team could not field enough players for a particular game. In fact, on the last day of the 1982 schedule, the team faced that very dilemma, a dilemma that had bedevilled the season that had preceded it. A spectator, the apparently perplexed brother of Blacks outfielder Steve Williams, was drafted. He may have begun the game by inquiring about its basic rules, an indication that the game was not to go too well. But, for reasons that were left unknown, Bob Williams managed a hit and two fairly decent fielding plays. Of course, the team eventually found a way to lose the game, thereby plunging team president and general manager into the dark contemplation that a record of five wins and fifteen losses can precipitate. A curious note. Bob Williams, brother of Steve who himself would go on to play for the Dukes for twelve seasons out of the next twenty years, would never again appear in a Duke game. I did, however, later join Bob as one of his teammates on a local fast pitch/slow pitch team almost thirty years later. I think the team was called the Knights although I could be wrong. Back in 1982, we gave Bob a nickname. We called him "The Comrade" or "The Commissar", a reference as I recall to the Soviet like cap that he was wearing when he played that one game for the Dukes.

Even the most uninitiated of observers could offer adequate summary of the Blacks' performance during the 1982 season: no hitting, no fielding, too few players, and at times, too many. Although the situation was not quite as turbulent as it had been during the 1981 season, during which the Blacks were known to arrive with seven players one game and seventeen the next, the theme of perpetual transition well established. Only the arguably solid pitching of Livingstone, Power and Yakabuski kept the bottom from completely falling out. Elsewhere, circumstances were unkind. The infield seemed to be in perpetual disarray, players exchanging errors like baseball cards. The outfield, sometimes a place of exile over which fly balls flew uncaught, seldom called for balls hit to them. "I may have it" become an explanation for everything.

So the Blacks/Dukes won only five of twenty games in 1982 and were tied at the bottom of the league with the Swingers, a full ten games behind the Astros who won fifteen games and swept through the playoffs to claim the first league championship. The Astros, a new team composed of players with whom few of the other teams were familiar. That team was blessed with the Pritchard family, which included two brothers and two cousins although I am not entirely sure of that. One of them, Dave Pritchard was easily the best hitter in the league, not only in 1982, when he apparently hit well over .500, but for the remainder of the decade. There were, however, suggestions that the team's score keepers were at times a little too liberal, counting walks, fielding choices, and errors as hits, unnaturally increasing batting averages. It was rumoured that the team batting average for that first year was well over,400. The team's ace was the team's workhorse, Gerry Pritchard while its first baseman, Rick Pritchard performed fielding miracles with a glove that looked like it belonged in Cooperstown. The other Pritchard, Mike, contributed by orchestrating the team's fortunes from the bench. Slugging third baseman Rocky Warren who, despite his difficulty in hitting the curve, was also a pivotal Astro while another important Astro was a guy named McCooeye who is remembered as a miraculous defensive player despite wearing unsightly thick spectacles and occasional odd behaviour.

At the opening Duke practice in the spring of 1983, held ironically enough in a parking lot full of snow, there was reason I recall to be optimistic. At least half a dozen members of the 1982 team, motivated it was assumed by the thought of repeating their unfortunate performances of the previous year, had decided to retired for less embarrassing pursuits. As replacements, my brother John, his scouting efforts ever adept, had assembled an impressive cast of recruits. However, even then, problems were already emerging. At least two guys who had advertised themselves as pitchers either could not pitch at all or could not pitch without hurting himself or the batter. In addition, there was a new first baseman who couldn't run and a new third basemen who wouldn't pay. Still, despite the loss of their best pitcher, the arrival of Greg and Steve Pearce as well as Dan and Rick Russell had the Dukes thinking playoff berth. And for a while, they could have expected more than that.

In their first game of the 1983 season, which was held in beautiful downtown Aylmer after both teams were unexpectedly prohibited from using the Lynda Lane diamond, the Dukes, resplendent in new navy and white uniforms, defeated the eventual league champion Swingers in a game highlighted by strong pitching and a home run by Jack Livingstone. In fact, by the sixth game of the year, they were sporting a record of four wins and two losses, looking very much like a team to be reckoned with. After all, they appeared to have a capable pitching staff in Jack Livingstone and the Russell brothers which, though weakened by the loss of Rob Power to a rival league, still kept the Dukes in most games. The infield seemed competent enough with Greg Pearce, Rick Russell and myself appearing most of the time. In addition, the outfield of Gary Lindfield, newcomer Steve Pearce and Steve Williams, who played together most of the time, were regarded, at least by team management, as among the league's best. With catcher Larry Johnson's mostly capable leadership as a final ingredient, speed and high decibel exhortations to teammates his primary talents, the Dukes, however unlikely, looked like a contender. The team even started to like their uniforms, which was surprising since, to tell you the truth, they looked like they might have belonged on East German volleyball players and had been purchased at a discount store.

Like all baseball slumps, the origins of our descent into mediocrity remained elusive, no matter how often the team discussed it during post-game libations. Theories and musings abounded, not that any of it mattered. Two of the team's best hitters, Steve Pearce and myself went into inexplicable declines. I myself struck out seven times in succession at one point, prompting many of the teammates to recommend psychiatric treatment. I remember claiming, with Cartesian aplomb, that "I stink, therefore I am." Nobody else on the team got it. I remember contemplating the concept of the strikeout while I was becoming so familiar with it. It is one of those things that makes baseball the most curious of athletic endeavours. It is more often than not measured out in failure rather than achievement, its parameters defined by a player's ability to avoid errors as often as possible. No other game is quite like it, no other sport so dependent on the efforts of its participants to avoid looking like complete fools. At the centre of this philosophical quandary, at the very heart of the game's facility to humiliate those who play it, is a strike out, a relatively simple act of waving helplessly at a thrown baseball. It is a commonplace failure, the kind of misfortune that befalls every player, an apparently guilt free transgression that improves with repetition, a failure with which all players can commiserate.

At the time, while I was going through the worst decline in my memory, dropping more than a hundred points from last year's batting average, my only bright spot being a legitimate triple that I hit at Tunney. Temporary though I hoped that my slump was, I actually contemplated retirement, my despair as obvious as the statistic that recorded its infamy. It could have been a reckoning that I would not have to face for another thirty years. My brother John, who had recently transferred to me his previous responsibilities as field manager, talked me out of it, claiming quite reasonably that he didn't have a suitable replacement. I also came to the realization, after surveying current major league batting statistics, that strikeouts were no longer the embarrassment that they were when I was in little league. In fact, it has only got worse or better, depending on your point of view. In a recent edition of *Sports Illustrated*, in an article decrying the slowing pace of major league baseball games, the reporter noted that over the course of four hours during which the Los Angles Dodgers beat the Milwaukee Brewers 2-1, 90 batters went to the plate and only 40 of them actually put the ball in play. Nine pitchers combined to strike out a National League record 42 batters. All three runs scored on solo home runs. One of the conclusions of the story was that the baseball has become obsessed with power; i.e. strikeouts by pitchers and home runs by batters. In retrospect, then, why should I have been particularly distressed by striking out seven times in a row? One final note. In 2016, Chris Davis of the Baltimore Orioles struck out 219 times. In comparison, sixty years before that, when my hero, Mickey Mantle happened to win the Triple Crown, he struck out 75 times, a couple months worth of strike outs for contemporary sluggers. And remember, Mantle was often criticized for striking out too much. Looking back, I should have taken the Alfred E Newman approach and not worried about it at all. Another final note. Over the more than twenty years I played for the Dukes, I must have had dozens of teammates who struck out with greater frequency than I did.

Aside from team offence, which was acceptable most of the time, the Pearce and Russell brothers as well as Larry Johnson and Gary Lindfield provided the best part of it, the team's defence in 1983 remained suspect to say the least, the main explanation it could be argued for their eventual record of eight wins and twelve losses. Fielders, who during the early part of the season were dependable enough, were suddenly seized by apparent strokes or temporarily crippled. Balls went through their legs, balls were dropped that could have been caught by a spaniel, they threw to the wrong bases. Pickoff plays became set pieces for keystone cop remakes as two and three base errors became commonplace. A mid-season recruit named Doug Bristol, claiming to have pitched somewhere in the minor leagues, immediately appeared to support the desultory story by demonstrating curious control problems. He also added to team history by tripping a Duke runner while coaching third base in the first game in which he appeared. Another mid-season pitching acquisition, a guy named Rob Sanderson, also couldn't find the plate with a GPS and a topographical map, walking ten batters and giving up twelve runs in only five innings. He did, however, have a great looking wife, fuelling strange speculation among envious teammates.

At that time, and many times since I would suggest, I contemplated the transgression of the baseball fielding error, no more a devastating statistic in any other sport than the humble fielding error in baseball. Running backs may fumble, quarterbacks may throw interceptions, hockey and basketball players may make errant passes, and tennis players may double fault but no other accident of fortune, misconception or miscalculation takes a more prominent place in the very structure of the game in which it occurs than the humble baseball error. It is a fundamental element of the game, immortalized on the scoreboard with the other two standard variables of the game, hits and runs. Actually recorded as an essential measure of the game, the error cannot be hidden or ignored in the trivia of a line score. The error stands alone as a singular fault horror. Somewhere along the line, every player, no matter how inconsequential his limitations, will encounter the error. It simply happens, a curse prepared to pounce on any innocent carrying a baseball glove. Not all errors, however, are created equal. Sure, they are accorded equal importance in the statistics, anonymously appearing as a single figure in box scores and the like. But they are remembered by their context, their effect on the historical importance of the game in which they occurred. Hence, reference is made to the misfortunes of first baseman Bill Buckner of Boston Red Sox whose well remembered error in game six of the 1986 World Series basically handed the game and ultimately the series to the New York Mets. Had Mr. Buckner made his miscue during a mid-season, a blowout loss to Seattle for example rather the game six of the 1986 World Series, then Mr. Buckner's career might have been celebrated differently.

Aside from their context, errors are also defined by the position and probably the character of the player making them. In the infield, the first baseman is universally regarded as a slugger type whose sole responsibility is to catch the ball and ensure that his foot is on the first base bag. He could easily be expected to blame another infielder for any fielding misfortune that may befall him, even if the throw he drops is a waist high lollipop that could have been caught by someone with a hood over his head. On ground balls, forget it. Hit it by the first baseman and only the most mean spirited scorer will call it an error. As a perverse result, errors by a first baseman, since their position seems comparatively easy to field and because they are often suspected of attempting to assign blame to a teammate, somehow seem more egregious than those by other fielders. This brings us to the second baseman, the shortstop and to a lesser extent, the third baseman. These players, more often than not, are the best fielders on the team. While they precipitate the majority of the team's miscues, they benefit from a certain sympathy from the other players. After all, they handle the most fielding chances and the most difficult fielding chances than any other player on the team and can often atone for any of their errors by making the most spectacular plays. Great shortstops may bounce on their heads to field a ball and can therefore expect forgiveness for the occasional blunder.

Outfielders, however, are not as fortunate. They are much more vulnerable to criticism should they misplay a ball. Not only does the outfield appear to be in an easy position to play but the consequences of any mistakes made there are usually more dramatic, Mr. Buckner's historic blunder notwithstanding. A shortstop screws up a grounder and a man is probably no further than first base. An outfielder drops a ball and a man could be on third. Moreover, outfielders, more than any other player, are often given to theatrical displays which can enrage the opposition with their spectacular plays but frighten the manager with their errors. The fielding histrionics pursued by past hot dogs like Ricky Henderson and current hot dogs like Kevin Pillar sometimes make their errors seem like poetic justice.

Pitchers and catchers are in a class by themselves, the latter because of the sympathy the burden of their position can generate and the former because of their occasional inability to do anything other than pitch. Pitchers are traditionally perceived as moody individuals, perhaps like prizefighters one supposes, all exposed nerve endings and concentration. They cannot hit, an assessment that hasn't changed much over the years, and may not be able to field, a characterization that is not universally accepted. Then there is the catcher, the ancient mariner of the diamond whose responsibilities may overwhelm him occasionally. Unlike any other defensive player, the catcher, facing away from the hitter as if in apprehension, usually finishes the game looking like he has been playing football, not baseball. The impact of the equipment the catcher wears, the fact that he is compelled to squat like a turtle for several hours, and the foul tips the catcher has to endure suggest that the catcher does not play the game, he survives it. The occasional passed ball or dropped foul ball can be overlooked, no penitence required, as if criticism would only compound his anxiety. On the other hand, throw too many balls into the outfield and a catcher can be expected to join his teammates in purgatory. Sometimes, however, criticism of specific misgivings can easily become epic, the example of Yankee catcher Gary Sanchez and his tendency to compile passed balls indicative.

For the individual player, perhaps the most important factor with respect to errors is his reaction after committing one. This is particularly typical for the recreational player, playing as he does in games where errors are so prevalent. One of the more popular approaches revolves around the basic avoidance syndrome. Under this scenario, the player committing the error simply pretends that it didn't happen. No bowed heads, no muttered curses, no suicidal gestures. You blow it and then react as if you didn't. If you manage to keep the errors at an acceptable minimum, this approach will usually work, particularly if your teammates have no other compelling reason, such as an excess of body odour or an admiration for Donald Trump, for hating your guts. An extreme variant of this technique has the guilty party hiding from the error rather than ignoring it. The practitioner of this tactic will invariably run off the field smiling as if nothing was amiss or, in more extreme cases, attempt to pull his cap over his head. This approach, however, is not recommended by most therapists.

Another popular, although entirely dissimilar, approach can be characterized as the emotional outburst method. This sensitive response, whether manifested in uncontrollable laughter, guilt ridden sobbing or a crazed burst of anger, may have its advantages, particularly if one is convincing enough to ensure that your teammates won't go near you for an inning or two. This approach is even more effective if you are known to have a history of emotional problems or have been or should be a convicted felon. Brandishing a handgun is an option here, but only if you're playing in South America. The other major technique of responding to the occasional inadequacy has some of the annoying properties of the other approaches. This kind of player acts like he cannot believe that he had made an error. He looks dumbfounded, as if a victim of a sudden conspiracy. The implication is clear enough. The player is simply too skilled to err, too proficient to allow a ball to slip through his legs. If that weren't enough, some of these players find the gall to demand, in an appropriately loud voice, that the next ball be hit to them, as if to prove that the error was a complete aberration.

I recall years later, when fielding percentages was introduced to the gallery of statistics that was recorded in the annual Duke magazine, consideration of errors became highly debatable among my teammates with some, particularly those whose gloves were, as the expression went, made of stone. Many objected to the inclusion of such potentially embarrassing information while less error prone players were appropriately ambivalent, if not agnostic about the stats. There was also considerable irony surrounding the recording of errors on the Dukes, a practice that lasted maybe ten years before it was happily retired. In addition to complaining about the recording of errors, many of my teammates tried to ensure that errors were so strictly defined that they could never be applied very often. One of my more litigious teammates, who otherwise had been a dependable and congenial teammate for many years, would often dispute the scoring of a ball that clearly went through his legs as an error, the opposite formulation that he employed when he had hit the ball through the legs of somebody on the other team. His often repeated explanation that the ball had eaten up either him or the other player, the meaning being that the ball had been hit so hard that only an extraordinary defensive play could have prevented it from getting by him. Years later, Duke alumni were still referring to the expression.

In my latter years as a Duke, those years when my sole role on the team was to sit on the bench, keep score and wonder what I could do to qualify for some playing time, a teammate made a particularly unmistakable error during a playoff game. His reaction to his error, he had been playing second base, was to fling his glove down, kick up some dust, and offer up a stream of expletives. He did not bother to pursue the ball that he had allowed to slip through his legs. None of my teammates admonished him for his behaviour, either then or later. And I was the player sitting on the bench like a piece of sculpture, a bobble head.

# INNINGS

I do recall that the team entered the last part of that second season with a reasonable chance of making the playoffs. However, while the team's hitting had returned, the errors, the walks allowed and the occasional base running blunder eventually ran us out of the playoff picture. Still, the Dukes managed to win eight games that season, a three game improvement over 1982. It was, however, a minimal improvement compared to the eight game advance by their fellow cellar dweller from the previous season, the Swingers who completed their ascension by winning the championship for 1983. They were led by another pair of brothers, the redoubtable Guzzos who would go on to led that team and others for years.

Those first two years of the Ottawa Recreational Baseball League were surprising in several ways. First of all, league games were officiated by carded umpires, compensated and administered in accordance with a provincial baseball umpire association. No longer would the games be managed by the players themselves but by objective arbitrators. That fact alone got me thinking at the time about the umpires with whom we had to deal at the time. To me, and this was a view that went down to my days in little league, they were the judges of summer, presumably ordinary mortals who were transformed through a ritual of rules into a final authority, beyond appeal, reproach or suggestion of error, as infallible as a Pope in the Middle Ages. They were impervious to pressure and the confusions of fate, above it all somehow, sharing with existentialism and Buddist monks the serenity of knowing that you are right all of the time. Beyond them, there is chaos. They are perfection in an imperfect world who make more unassailable decisions in one game than a federal judge may make in a year. They may be analyzed, assessed and abused but remain invulnerable. They are islands of reason. They are baseball umpires.

Despite such apparent omnipotence, the umpire is hardly uniform in characteristic. Umpires, not unlike doctors for example, actually have personalities, a truth that usually eludes most players. Most young ballplayers, even those who are destined to go on to play at higher levels, can likely recall the first umpire they ever saw as being a beery old gent with a red nose and a tattered old baseball cap. Though hardly exemplary of the species in general, these geezers, who were sometimes presumed to have slept at the diamond, ate out of fast food bags, and eventually died of exposure once winter set in, were usually amiable Casey Stengel types whose sometime elusive grasp of the rules did not prevent them from passing on to their young charges an appreciation and respect for their wisdom, if not the game. Along that line, one memorable umpire from those early years was an older, possibly geriatric gentleman named Jerry Wallace, a man who commanded immediate veneration, no matter how unpredictable the conduct of his duties. It did not matter, for example, if Mr. Wallace sometimes applied a strike zone which extended from the ankles to the chin. Wallace may have looked to some of us like a Santa Claus down on his luck. Even the most cynical little leaguer would have been reluctant to pass critical commentary to an old man who might be in a position to ensure that you didn't get anything for Christmas. Wallace had a number of other strange habits. For example, he would occasionally halt a game to explain to befuddled players the machinations of the balk and then relate some humorous though irrelevant memory. No one argued with him, unsure as to whether he would in fact understand their objections. When he passed away, the funeral home viewing attracted a large crowd of players. League divisions and trophies were named after him.

In those first two seasons, we were introduced to a number of other types of umpires. One of the two senior umpires, aside from Mr. Wallace, was a courtly gentleman named John Jordan, the type of umpire who seemed better qualified to sit on the federal bench than officiate at a humble baseball game. Equipped with an unnatural quality of wisdom it seemed, Mr. Jordan made the most controversial judgment seem unavoidable somehow, almost inevitable, as if a strike three call on a ball that bounced on the plate was beyond reproach or comment. Umpires like Jordan often developed a kind of sure handed dominance over a game that made challenges to their calls permanently misguided. Players under their charge may have regarded such umpires as surrogate priests or teachers, so complete was their reputation. Besides, umpires like Mr. Jordan spoke softly and carried no stick. He also had respectable silver hair. Like Jerry Wallace, he too was commemorated by the league through the naming of divisions and trophies after him.

Another major category of umpires, at least in terms of my admittedly unscientific observations, was the friendly type. Such umpires seemed to enjoy calling a game simply because it beats staying home and watching television. They seemed bound to endlessly socialize with the players. They were forever deliberating with anyone who would listen, chatting up players from both teams with equal enthusiasm, pursuing anecdotes with the elan of a talk show host, a running chronology of comment coming out of him like the annoying neighbour next door. To such umpires, the game seemed somehow tangential. They were apathetic to its form and outcome. In fact, some were almost existential in their approach. "So what." they would claim, "I've just blown another call." Most players were almost inured to their comic indifference. Compared to the threat of nuclear war, for example, erroneous strike calls by a fast talking, overly congenial umpire just wasn't worth the trouble of disputing them. Another observation. Such umpires were often unwilling, maybe even unable to throw anyone out of a game, regardless of provocation. On the other hand, such umpires, their smiling demeanour perpetually intact, were seldom given the chance.

Any discussion of umpires and umpiring would not be comprehensive without consideration of the General Patton school of officiating. These individuals, who appeared to have received their training in a military boot camp, combine the assertiveness of the military with the quiet diplomacy of an armed robber. They were profoundly combative umpires who seemed to take great delight in calling you out, always it seemed with a sneer on their faces. During those earliest two years of the ORBL, there was one umpire whose name I think may have been Preston. He was quite assertive in his behaviour, calling the game as if he was commanding troops on parade. One small episode worth recounting. He was the only umpire who ever threw me out of a game. It was the result of my objection to his decision to call me out for allegedly stepping on the plate while hitting. While I had no doubt that Mr. Preston or whatever his name was correct on the rule, I insisted that my foot was not on the plate anyway. For stating that contention, umpire Preston immediately threw me out of the game. I cannot recall whether there were any further recriminations for my behaviour which was surprising in view of the future history of the administration of league discipline. Looking back, I never could explain my behaviour at the time.

There were several other developments in those first two years that contributed to the evolution of the league and the team. Aside from all the administrative details of running a nascent baseball league, schedules, teams fees, statistics, that kind of thing, there were two other changes from the semi-organized sandlot baseball that proceeded it. In one of the many obligations that my brother John, as de facto commissioner of the league, imposed on the league was the requirement that teams wear uniforms, actual uniforms that allowed players to recognize their own teammates. There were, however, arguments against the necessity for baseball players requiring uniforms. Unlike football, hockey and basketball players, where uniforms were usually necessary, baseball players seldom, if ever, confuse the opposition with their own teammates. Given the structure of the game, even if such a colossal mistake were to be made, not that I have ever seen or heard of such an error, what possible difference would that make anyway? Of the six teams that played over those first two seasons, the usage of uniforms was haphazard to say the least. The 1982 Astros wore jerseys that featured the name of the team sponsor, "Holmes Heating" emblazoned across their chests while the 1983 champion Swingers, which were or were likely to be sponsored by a local business "Estra Flooring", also went with their name slashed across the front of their jerseys. There was no consistency regarding the placing of sponsor names on the uniforms of the other teams in the league, that is if they were sponsored. But for the Red Eyes, who wore humble t-shorts but were sponsored by one of the most celebrated watering holes in the city, "Le Chateau Lafayette", the remaining teams in the league all wore matching uniforms. Those other three in the leagues, the Dukes, the Sun Devils, and the Sweat Sox, were or were soon to be sponsored by the "Dukes of Somerset" bar, the "Blue Bayou" restaurant, and "Pete & Mary's", a local pub. I cannot be certain that these histories are entirely accurate although there is likely enough truth for this commentary. As for the Dukes, we wore relatively cheap blue and white t-shirts/pant combos, my only complaint at the time that the font on the t-shirts was a little small and archaic, the latter reflecting the old fashioned nature of the sponsoring bar and making visible recognition of any sponsor difficult in any event.

At the end of that second season, a league banquet, which was more like a stag drinking session to be honest, was held in the basement of a church somewhere on Walkley Road. Someone had the presence of mind to obtain a permit to dispense liquor, a lot of guys got drunk, awards were announced although I don't think actual trophies were handed out, and it was rumoured that someone had absconded with the take from the sales of booze, my brother being convinced for years that he knew who the perpetrator was, his conclusion affirmed when the alleged thief was never seen again. My brother's efforts to organize and run the league for those two years was recognized by the league when he was presented with a baseball signed by as many players still sober enough to hold a pen that night. I remember that John was not impressed enough to keep the gift, later claiming that he had left it in that church basement. Finally, on that evening, I distributed to my teammates the first edition of the Duke magazine, a seventeen page record of the fortunes of the 1983 team. Produced by my brother and I on an ancient Underwood typewriter with the larger font titles inserted with Letraset, it included a story on the season just past, portraits of all fourteen guys who played for the team, a contrived interview with ORBL Commissioner Robertson and some rudimentary statistics. It was the first of many edition, the finale being published 28 years later, a season in which I was charitably allowed five plate appearances, the ultimate result being two base hits, the second being the last and 255$^{th}$ of my career in the now flourishing National Capital Baseball League.

# A KIND OF RESPECTABILITY

It was remarkable achievement actually. Within three years, the endeavour that my brother John had founded and nourished had succeeded beyond all expectation. After its obvious success in 1983, a season in which it managed to extend the achievements of its maiden season, the Ottawa Recreational Baseball League expanded from six to eight teams in 1984, from one division to two, and from a 60 to a 96 game schedule. The two new teams, the Dill Pickle Indians and the Frito Lay Fanatics, both immediately proved that they were shrewd additions to the league, offering both competition on the field and amiability off of it. In fact, so competitive were the Indians that they took the league title, winning six of eight playoff games. In so doing, they swept both my Dukes and the Sun Devils in straight games before encountering the Red Eyes who managed to extend the Indians to the maximum before submitting. A curious irony that a team that would win the league championship that year would be its only year in the league, its departure in 1985 almost preordained, predictable for a team that was apparently compromised almost entirely of university football players.

Otherwise, the 1984 season was a success without qualification. Despite the addition of the two new teams, the overall quality of the competition was much improved, or so it appeared, at least according to casual commentary from most of the players. With the Senior Interprovincial League seemingly on the brink of disintegration, losing teams and players while the ORBL was doing the reverse, the league was ready to assume the position of the premier baseball league in the city. While attendance to recreational league baseball games was hardly any indication of the popularity, if not the credibility of the league, I recall that over a hundred people showed up to take in the league's mid-season all-star game, an excellent game in which the Jordan Division team edged the representatives from the Wallace Division 6-5. I think I probably played in that game and may have contributed a hit and two flawless fielding plays. I also remember somebody hit a home run and several base runners were thrown out attempting to steal, courtesy of the prowess of new Swinger catcher Terry Brennan.

At the end of the previous season, a season during which the Dukes struggled to a record of eight wins and twelve losses to finish out of the playoffs for the second consecutive year, my brother and I handed off our responsibilities to relative newcomer Doug Bristow whose approach to baseball team management had resulted in the assignment of the moniker "Little General". Mr. Bristow, who was soon to enter the hierarchy of Duke legend even though he was a Duke for little more than two seasons, had joined the Dukes part way through the previous season, his introduction to the team memorialized by his tripping a Duke base runner from the third base coaching box. There was little doubt at the time that Bristow was well qualified to be officially designated a "character". There were his collection of often repeated baseball aphorisms and other forms of strange patter; his improbable stories about his career as a minor league pitcher, claiming at one point that several future Montreal Expos had been his teammates; his insistence on employing a complex system of signs which most of the team routinely ignored, and a career as an encyclopedia salesman.

In appointing Bristow manager, his relief palatable, my brother suggested that the 1984 Dukes would be at least three wins better than they had been in 1983. Happily enough as it turned out, the Dukes managed to exceed that lofty prognostication by winning four more games, a record that was good enough to propel them to second place in the Wallace Division, three games behind the first place Swingers. By way of comparison, the team could well have been satisfied that their performance, which for the first time had them winning as many games as they lost. On the other hand, the Dukes closed out the season by losing four straight, including their two playoff games to the eventual league champion Dill Pickle Indians. Disappointment was obvious. The Dukes had approached the 1984 season with considerable enthusiasm. Unlike the two previous years, when their prospects were subdued, if not dreary, when presumably pessimistic Duke management invariably faced the unenviable task of replacing half the roster, the team entered the season virtually intact, only having lost one of their pitchers, Rob Sanderson who moved to Toronto with his nice looking wife. As a replacement, Rob Power, after toiling somewhat unhappily in the Senior Interprovincial League, returned to take up his previous duties as the team's best pitcher.

New manager Bristow had begun the 1984 campaign by initiating indoor practice sessions in January, unheard preparation for a team that had not only lost more than twice as many games than it had won over the previous two years but actually had trouble in assembling a team for opening day. There was a certain reluctance about attending manager Bristow's winter practices, the cynicism of most Dukes not allayed by the "Little General"'s predictable approach to practice, which seemed to be based more on the prescriptions of a drill sergeant than a baseball coach. Nevertheless, attendance, which may have been based more on the post-practice pursuit of libations than any sense of preparation for the impending season, remained steady enough, even for the intense Bristow, who was astute to ignore the lack of enthusiasm, if not the comic insouciance occasionally shown by most of his charges.

Given the team's performance during the short exhibition schedule as well as during the first few regular seasons games, optimism, hardly a customary notion for a team as accustomed to losing as the Dukes, seemed well founded. They seemed to have all the elements they thought necessary for success: four competent, if not veteran pitchers, including a rookie with the unlikely surname of Wudwud, which a lot of his teammates thought was a typographical error; an absurdly deep infield with ten Dukes with infield experience; and an already excellent outfield of Lindfield, Pearce and Williams which was augmented by an occasional appearance of John Pole, a pesky rookie who specialized in annoying umpires and engaging in legendary man-about-town hi-jinks. Regarding Mr. Pole, although relegated to batting an embarrassing .138 in that first year, he would later go on to become one of the best Duke players of all time in his fifteen years with the team. He also was responsible for applying the moniker of "the Worm" to teammate Steve Williams, a burden that Williams carried for decades it seemed.

Alas, while they continued to improve in 1984, gaining four games in the win column and reaching the .500 mark for the first time, they were rudely and decisively eliminated by the eventual champion Dill Pickle Indians in straight games in the quarter-finals. Despite their obvious excellence both on the mound led by the prodigal Rob Rower and at the plate where three Dukes, Larry Johnson, Greg Pearce and Rick Russell all hit over.400, the team's descent into disappointment was due for the most part to their old friend, the error, a statistic that was beginning to become synonymous with the Duke franchise. Again, as announced by the team periodical that year, the team would have to wait for next year.

I cannot recall where the league banquet was held that year. It might have been transferred to a DND hall as league commissioner Robertson had recently joined the department and apparently had access to any number of its facilities for such events. The team did, however, enjoy a team barbecue at the home of the one of the players, a festivity that would eventually become a team tradition. Wives, girlfriends and some children attended, some of whom had actually gone to some of the games. No one knew why.

As observed by the 1985 edition of the magazine, the expected script for the next season seemed simple enough. With the departure of the 1984 champion Dill Pickle Indians, the 1985 season would finally be the one which would confirm the inevitable ascent of the Red Eyes, which narrowly lost in the two previous champion series. After all, the Red Eyes, which were a unique combination of good players wearing lousy uniforms, simply ran out of gas against the Indians in last year's finals and the Swingers in the finals of the year before. With the Indians gone, their players departing for presumably more lucrative pursuits, the Red Eyes had to be considered the favourites for 1985. And for much the season, there seemed to be little doubt of an inevitable triumph. That is until they ran into the Swingers, the 1983 champions, in the finals. Prior to the series, the Red Eyes sported a record of 22 wins in 24 games, far and away the best record in the league's four year history. Still, despite the probability and their record, the Red Eyes, after winning two of the first three games in the finals, proceeded to lose the next two games, thereby ceding the championship to the Swingers who won for the second time in three years. The Red Eyes were a team anchored by pitchers Terry Kealy who won thirteen and lost only one game and Kevin Levya who turned in a similar record, winning eight and losing the only other game the team lost that year. Aside from the two pitchers, another Red Eye keystone was Bob Yanus, the well known ancient mariner of Ottawa baseball who apparently was playing baseball in the city since the end of World War II. As for the champion Swingers, they were fortunate enough to have a bevy of superior ball players in the Guzzo brothers, Fred and Sam, Ray Licari, Tony Constantini, catcher Terry Brennan and a surprisingly nimble first baseman and well beloved though unfortunately deceased chef named Giovanni Leo.

As had been the case every year since its establishment, the 1985 season was another unqualified success. According to the league's umpires, the overall quality of the play continued to improve, despite the addition of one new team to replace the Indians. That team was sponsored by an Elgin Street bistro named Maxwell's. Again, the league organization remained sound with all eight teams expected to return the next year. Its reputation as a viable baseball league within the city was so enhanced that the league was finding it relatively easy to obtain permits to use the city's baseball diamonds. Although the league again failed to generate much spectator interest, most games being attended by more players than fans, events such as the second annual all-star game, which maybe 150 fans witnessed, demonstrated that the league continued to have a future. Furthermore, maybe a hundred potential recruits showed up at a tryout camp at Lynda Lane held before the season began. While I cannot report on the number of recruits picked up by teams looking for players, the Dukes did introduce new two names to the team biography, a future Ottawa city manager named Steve Kanalakas and a friend of catcher Larry Johnson named George Zegarec. Neither rookie played more than one season with the team.

There were several incidents during the 1985 season which could easily have qualified for permanent placement in team history. The pursuit of a team record was the heart of the matter when one of the fastest Dukes, at one time the career leader in stolen bases, in an attempt to establish a new single season record, refused to run beyond first base on any ball hit anywhere in the last several games of the season. He also declined to run from first on failed pick off attempts, passed balls, or wild pitches. He did not, however, break the record, a record set in 1984 and still held by catcher Larry Johnson. Another Duke, who only played that year, fell asleep during a Sunday morning game at Britannia Park, awoke after the game and had the audacity to ask whether he missed anything.

The end of the 1985 season was blessed with a banquet held in a hall out among the barracks in Uplands. For the first time, league trophies were handed out, in both team and individual categories, the latter actually voted on by the players themselves. In that context, I must admit that I was surprised, if not shocked by receiving the award for the most improved player, a trophy that is still sitting on my dresser at home. I have long assumed that I had earned the accolade by hitting .333, improving my batting average by some 75 percentage points from the previous two seasons. It is interesting to note that while the league handed out five awards that year, most valuable player, best pitcher, best batting average, most improved, and the championship, it is possible that several dozen honours were distributed in the most recent year, the obvious result of expanding from eight teams in two divisions in 1985 to 37 teams in four tiers in 2017.

As for the Dukes, that sublime maxim coined by Mr. Lawrence Berra about not being over until it's over is particularly relevant. While one is relatively assured that Yogi was not quoted after the second game of the opening round of the playoffs between the Dukes and their longtime nemesis, the Sun Devils, many of the Dukes who were present were to remember it. For this was a game in which the Dukes showed an emotional depth not previously evident, thereby ending a mediocre year in which they lost two more games than they won. It was a game which the Dukes could easily have entered with the resignation of condemned men. They had endured a bitterly disappointing loss in game one of the series, a contest in which the team saw a carefully constructed 4-2 lead suddenly evaporate on the strength of consecutive home runs in the bottom of the ninth inning. They then lost it outright in the tenth inning on a two out, two strike suicide squeeze. Despair seemed too flippant a term.

For the Dukes, the second game seemed less the final defeat of yet another disappointing season than some sort of vindication of its character. As a game, it had almost an embarrassment of theatrics: in the field, where catcher Larry Johnson managed to throw out two base runners, Steve Williams had four outfield assists, which were likely more than he or any other Duke had all season, and I somehow made an unassisted double play with the bases loaded in the ninth inning; and at the plate, where Gary Lindfield, easily the best that the Dukes had to offer in 1985, placing second in league batting behind perennial batting champion Dave Pritchard of the Astros, came through with three base hits on the evening. But it was the Duke comeback in the latter innings that led to the ascension of the game into Duke mythology. The Dukes had fallen behind the Sun Devils by five runs, specifically 8-3 by the eighth inning, when the Dukes erupted for five runs to tie the score going into the ninth inning. In the bottom of that inning, they easily could have won the game, loading the bases with one out, only to ground into a force out at the plate and then watching with abject horror as Lindfield struck out on three hellish curve balls from Sun Devil pitcher and future league commissioner Jim Dean. The Duke despair deepened when Lindfield dropped a likely double play ball in the top of the tenth inning. Instead of being out of the inning, the Dukes allowed the Sun Devils to score six more runs and took the game going away. A final legendary misfortune. Gary Lindfield, now undeniably a tragic, if not inconsolable figure, left the McCarthy field after the final Duke out without speaking or even acknowledging any of his teammates.

Many of his teammates may have thought that he had departed. I don't think anyone but me ever saw Mr. Lindfield again. I saw him maybe 25 years later. He contacted me at work to solicit a donation to a fund supporting some sort of investigation into the case of a murdered relative. I forgot if I made a donation.

There were a number of interesting developments that emerged before and during the 1986 season of the Ottawa Recreational Baseball League. For the third successful year, the league added new teams to the league, bringing league membership to ten teams. The new entrants, the Athletics and Las Palmas stumbled to predictably unenviable records of 7-20 and 1-26 respectively. For the first time in league history, the league publication, the venerable *Baseball Ottawa,* published accounts, complete with photographs and biographical commentaries, of all 157 players on all ten teams in the league. While appreciative, some of the players in the league predictably thought the publishers/editors/writers could have used some editorial guidance. As always, the enterprise was produced by John and I on an old manual Underwood typewriter, with Letreset lettering, scotch tape, and a gallon of whiteout. The popularity of the publication was such that we felt compelled to continue to publish a league *Baseball Ottawa* for another four years, finally giving way to another editorial team who distributed a league magazine for three years after that.

By that time, while magazine production was much less arduous than it had been previously, the use of PCs and digital photographs having obvious advantages, there were many more teams in the league, up to 30 teams by 1992, which made reporting on them a journalistic nightmare, particularly since few of our colleagues in the league seemed to be willing to contribute anything to the enterprise. By then, John, who had retired as league commissioner after the 1986 season and was reluctant to continue any duties aside from playing occasionally, was admittedly relieved to give up any obligation to anyone else to publish a league magazine. Regardless, for reasons that I cannot recall, loyalty and altruism possible explanations, both of us continued to produce a team magazine for a few more years, after which time I took over it on my own, a tradition to which I seemed to have been masochistically addicted until I left the team for good in 2010.

As for the 1986 season itself, the Red Eyes, who had been disappointed in three of the championship finals, finally broke through to win their first league championship. Observers all agreed that it just had to happen; called it inevitability, some sort of manifest destiny. The Red Eyes had been in the finals in the three previous years and came up short on all three occasions. They had won over ninety percent of their games over the past two years, including 22 out of 27 games in 1986. They had hit .330 as a team in 1986, a mark which was better than at least 75 percent of the batting averages posted by all the players in the entire league. In addition, four of their regular players hit over .400 while their pitching, despite the loss of last year's ace Terry Kealey, relied on Kevin Levya and Bob Chevrier who pitched 80 percent of the team's innings in 1986 and went 18-4 between them. All of this and they also had the theatrical personalities of Bill Polisek and Bob "the Buff" Yanus to help them out. Still, in the semi-finals of the playoffs, the Red Eyes were barely able to beat the Dukes, who lost almost three times as many games as the Red Eyes had in the regular season and may have won that series if Dukes pitching sensation John Pole not been injured and lost for game three of that series.

Despite losing their best player, the silently spectacular Gary Lindfield, as well as their unnecessarily intense manager Doug "The Little General" Bristow, before the 1986 season even started, the Dukes managed to stay afloat long enough to beat the Sun Devils in the playoff quarterfinals and throw a scare into the Red Eyes in the next round. They had added a guy named Dick Bondy who turned out to be probably the best player the Dukes had ever recruited up until that point, both at the plate and on the mound. There was the emergence of Tom Wudwud as the team pitching ace and the best season I have ever had playing any kind of baseball. I authored 30 base hits that season, placed second in the league batting average, and fielded first base as if I actually knew where the balls were going. Aside from the relative success of that season, its best since the league was established in 1982, the team did stagger out of the gate as the season started. They faced several dilemmas. They had to replace Lindfield, eventually finding a replacement in Dick Bondy. Manager Bristow resigned from the team a week before the season began after a memorably bizarre incident at a pre-season practice. Known for running unusually strict practices that seemed more akin to football than baseball, insisting on wind sprints, endless infield drills, bunting practice, but no batting practice which I had to admit was generally a waste of time anyway. No, it was his instruction, if not his insistence about signs from base coaches that prompted the controversy. In the two years that Bristow managed the Dukes, his repeated attempts to convince his players to actually pay attention to signs from base coaches, the responsibility for which was usually rotated among the players, their own reluctance unmistakable, were generally ignored. Very few of my teammates were even remotely acquainted with the importance of signs to the game of baseball. I must admit that when I remembered, I would pay attention to signs although I eventually gave up after I realized that most of my teammates did not even know the signs and were not paying attention to any of them anyway. I recall executing a sacrifice bunt that led to a double play when both base runners seemed to be unaware that the bunt play was on. This understandably led to considerable frustration on manager Bristow's part. Sometimes, I thought he was going to break into tears on those occasions during which his gyrations in the third base coach's box resulted in not only neglect but prompted ridicule from his own team.

According to Bristow, this kind of wanton disregard for one of the most treasured traditions of the game could lead to anarchy. Bristow admitted though that there was nothing aesthetically satisfying about pulling on his earlobe several hundred times a game. In any event, Bristow had the team huddle up at some point during that fateful practice and then informed them that he would resign from the team if it didn't start paying attention to his instructions, particularly as they related to coaching signs. There was a brief silence and then maybe two or three guys agreed, a statement that immediately elicited serious laughter from most of the team. A shocked look came over his face, he made a classic "turn on his heel" move and headed toward the parking lot. One of our more loquacious teammates looked at John and I and informed us that we would soon taking over the team — again. As the season developed, it became clear that I would be managing the team, at least for the rest of the season. It wasn't my first turn at the job.

It was during the 1986 season that the local CTV station ran a news story about the league, interviewing on camera my brother John, Fred Guzzo of the Swingers and myself. The story was videotaped at the Britannia Park diamond during a game between the Swingers and the Dukes. It ran on CJOH three days later. Not surprisingly, I taped the story but the video I made of the spot was misplaced sometime during the last 31 years. Not surprising but a pity nonetheless. I often wonder if anyone else actually remembers. Funny, I also seem to remember that it was that year that league standings started to appear in the *Ottawa Citizen*. I don't know how long that lasted. Even though there are now more than three times as many teams as there were in 1986, there haven't been any statistics or any other information for that matter published by either of the Ottawa newspapers for some time. I cannot explain it.

Prior to and since the Ottawa Recreational Baseball League (ORBL) was officially established in 1982, they were playing under the shadow of local little leagues and then more importantly, the Senior Interprovincial

Baseball League (SIBL), an older and supposedly more reputable adult league. The ORBL and its antecedents, those guys who played pick up baseball on the Lynda Lane diamonds since the late 1970s, were always struggling with those leagues for access to those diamonds, a process that sometimes involved the police, and through a city administration that ritualistically denied issuing permits for playing on the those two and other fields. In the subsequent few years, after insistent lobbying by league commissioner John Robertson, the city finally relented and started issuing permits to use the local diamonds. Still, while the SIBL continued to hold the upper hand in local baseball, it may have been losing its grip on superiority. The two leagues had started playing all star games, they were conducting an interlocking schedule, and players were casually transferring from one league to another. Then, just prior to the opening of the 1987 season and after lengthy and often misunderstood negotiations, an entire team, the Ottawa Nepean Canadians, erstwhile champions of the SIBL, joined the Ottawa Recreational Baseball League. In view of their reputation and the reputation of the league they were leaving, there was a certain apprehension about the Canadians among the teams in the recently renamed Ottawa Baseball League (OBL).

Despite their pedigree, the Canadians did not have a particularly easy time winning their first OBL championship, which they did in their first season in the league. They stumbled out of the block, winning only one of their first five games, before ensuring that the trend did not continue, winning fifteen of their final twenty games before going undefeated in the first two rounds of the playoffs. Led by young strikeout artists Todd Burke and Garth Banning and three or four young sluggers, including a couple of recent graduated eighteen year olds from the Pinecrest Big League, the Canadians rolled into the finals against the Red Eyes with high, apparently justified expectations. It was during the finals that the Canadians and last year's champions, the Red Eyes, went the distance in a classic series. This was a five game series during which at least three games were authentic routs and at least one was a classic, one of the most exciting games in OBL history. Overall, the game, which ended in a 3-2 win by the Canadians, had it all, particularly great pitching by Brian Loughran of the Red Eyes and Banning and Burke of the Canadians, spectacular defensive plays, including six attempted steals successfully thrown out, and at least two circus catches in the outfield. Predictably, the deciding game of the series proved anti-climatic with the Canadian prevailing 7-4, a result that was less the dramatic finale than the previous playoff game promised.

Although they didn't make the playoffs in 1987, the Dukes managed to fashion the best record in their six year history, five games over .500, winning four games more than the previous year. Some suggested that their generally low batting average with only two Dukes, Steve Pearce and newcomer Andy Thompson, hitting over .300, and one of the worst fielding records in the league may have been an explanation. There were, however, several comic highlights over the Duke season. A particularly zany personality was a newcomer named Eddie Audet, a military man whose family owned a string of strip clubs and who could swear in at least three languages. It was Private Audit's only season with the Dukes, his whereabouts after that one season unknown. As for me, my season started badly and didn't get much better. I ended up, at my own insistence, on the bench for much of the year. I ended up with a third as many hits as I managed the last year, my batting average plunging by more than 200 points. Overall, it was an embarrassment.

In 1988, expansion entrant Kanata Selects became the twelfth team in the OBL. It also became the only team in league history to have what you could call widespread community support. They had a large supply of young players upon which to draw and a solid financial base on which to sustain a franchise. Despite such advantages, the team won only six games, a record that improved considerably over the next few years and maintained an exemplary record for the next two decades or so. As for the other teams in the 1988 season, the Red Eyes won their second championship in three years, beating the surprising Fanatics who ended up in the finals despite a relatively uninspiring regular season record. The Dukes tied the expansion Kanata for the worst record in the league and the worst record in their history, winning only six of 27 games. It was a nightmare season, the kind of season that prompted a multitude of explanations, none of which were particularly comforting. The Dukes generally got decent hitting but horrendous fielding, sometimes making as many as ten errors a game. Frequently recalled was one particularly egregious miscue when during a record four or five minute rundown between third base and home plate, every single Duke on the field handling the ball at least once, including all three Duke outfielders. A run eventually scored when two Dukes collided. These misfortunes reached a nadir of sorts during the season, sleepwalking to a 20-3 loss to the Sun Devils, a game that probably set new standards for a team that often regarded its failures as folklore. I too joined my Duke teammates in exploring the depths of baseball incompetence, hitting a little over the dreaded Mendoza line of .200. At the season ending barbecue, there was much discussion among disappointed Dukes about the need for serious changes if the Dukes were going to improve in 1989. John and I considered encouraging recent editions Andy Thompson and Dan Nicholls, both graduates of local big leagues, a singular characteristic of the latter being that he drove an army surplus jeep, to recruit any of their former teammates to join the Dukes next year. We were serious at the time. We even distributed questionnaires about the future of the team, hoping for support for fundamental changes to the team. Some of my teammates asked, with a certain understandable cynicism, for good seats on the bench. They thought we were joking.

The next season, the 1989 Dukes rebounded impressively from their disastrous finish of the previous year to make the playoffs for the first time in three years. Although they succumbed in the first round after throwing a scare into the eventual league champion Red Eyes, the 1989 Dukes showed enough promise to motivate even the most cynical observer to forget their woes of 1988 when they lost three times as many games as they won. The team was sure as hell a team in transition, having added six big league graduates in 1989 and 1988, all of whom were forming the nucleus of a team. It was now a team that sported only three starters from their 1986 playoff team. Despite the offensive heroics of newcomers Neil Campbell, Kevin Smyth, and Vinnie Wong, two of whom exemplified their youth by having their parents paying their team fees and all of whom hit well over .300, no one else on the team hit over .260. Although the hitting was shaky and the fielding even worse, the team admittedly had great pitching, a staff having cut more than three earned runs a game off the Duke pitching record stats of 1988. Still it wasn't enough for the Dukes even though they did manage to extend the Red Eyes in the first round of the playoffs.

# INNINGS

Despite the improvement, it was not worth the effort for more than half the team. After years of maintaining a roster of twelve or thirteen players, the Dukes suddenly had a team of nineteen players, with many fighting for playing time. The younger Dukes were central to the team's success and more or less had to and/or demanded to play every game. Of these, only one player, the team's best pitcher Don Nitchke, did not come to the plate that often, one of the few who preferred to have a designated hitter bat for him. That left a number of players who expected to play all the time, with at least two of them making it clear to team management that they had to start every game or they would be absent for the next game. In one particularly egregious display of petulance, a veteran Duke refused to even sit with his teammates after being pencilled into a game as a designated hitter. He then proceeded to strike out four consecutive times, intentionally as was suspected by his beach warming associates. I was tempted of course to respond to his antics by throwing him off the team. I was advised, however, that two of his friends, both starters, would join him in exile if I went through with any such decision. I should have anyway. Ironically enough, the moody designated hitter and his two friends never played for the Dukes after that season.

As manager that year, I felt like I was operating a daycare full of squabbling children. In addition, both John and I were, in effect, placed into the suspended animation of semi-retirement when we, somewhat pointless I now realize, sacrificed our own playing time for teammates who were not as charitable. Some simply stopped showing up for games or, like a couple of enterprising guys, got themselves ejected from games on purpose. A couple of players even suggested that since every player were supposed to pay an identical fee to play on the team, that is if they paid at all, every player should have the same amount of playing time. When that proposal was ignored, with a certain amount of whimsy, particularly by those who started the games, the same two players proposed that the amount of the fee for each individual player be based on that individual player's playing time. That proposition was also quietly abandoned although one of two enterprising Dukes produced a chart which showed that most of the starting players were paying about $2 for each plate appearance while many of the others were playing anywhere up to $20 for the same privilege.

I don't think that anyone other than those who did not get into many games saw the chart.

So, during that season, with so many players on the Duke roster, there were often more than a few not playing. In other words, they were "riding the pine" as it is often referred to in baseball vernacular. At times, there were more players "riding the pine" than playing in the game. Every baseball team seems to be burdened with them. They are the unused players consigned to perpetual contradiction. They are partial pariahs who, although ostracized from the rest of the team for the most part, are still expected to spectate with some enthusiasm. They sit on the bench like forlorn bystanders as the game swirls around them, unaffected by their presence and unconcerned about their fate. They are presumably alone in their thoughts, expected to cheer on the same teammates who, obviously more valuable to the team than they, perpetuate their lowly status. They are sometimes moody, sometimes deeply glum but sometimes overwhelmed with the thought that they might actually get into the game. But generally, they remain like passengers on a bus, supposedly stoic to their fate, unhappy with their lot, forgotten riders. In 1989, the Dukes had plenty of them.

Unlike other team sports, baseball provides the little used player with avenues of explanation through which he can escape his embarrassment, if not his dismay. For much of the season, major league teams dress 25 players. In September, they can dress as many as 40 players. With nine or ten players actually playing and five or six others vacationing in the bullpen, as many as ten other players are not engaged in the game in any capacity, more come September 1. Such players sit in the dugout like orphans. In the old days, they used to smoke cigarettes. Now they chew on sunflower seeds and still spit a great deal. Baseball, with its leisurely pace and timeless and relaxed demeanour, does not unduly penalize the bench warmer. There is sufficient compensation for whatever misery such players may feel.

Other sports may not be so kind. Hockey, with its frantic action and frequent player changes, isolates the little used player by either placing him at the end of the bench where he can advise the trainer on stick taping techniques or in the press box where he may trade witty observations with journalists on their fourth beer. Basketball is similar although given the proximity of the player bench to the spectators, the little used player, while much taller or differently dressed than most season ticket holders, could just as easily be a fan. There is football, with its fourty odd players milling about on the sidelines in confusing configurations: offence, defence, nickel packages, special teams. The unused player has few options. He can sit back from the action cradling his helmet, stand up with one of the coaches, exchange hand signals with players on the field, or, if he is real lucky, get to hold a clipboard for one of the coordinators.

But baseball is different. For much of the time, those riding the pine cannot be readily distinguished from those who are actually playing. Whether the team is on the field or at bat, there are enough players on the bench at any one time to overlook any one player's individual status. It is just not that obvious. Throw a few coaches in, particularly those coaches who are below retirement age and it is almost impossible to tell anyone apart. There are, however, several clues to identifying those who are playing to those who are not. The look on the face, the tenor of the conversation as well as the condition of the uniform usually can provide fairly convincing evidence. No matter what the surface, turf, grass or that awful gravel that cities often force on amateur baseball teams, players actually in the game, even if the uniform itself was in pristine condition, are always tugging at them in some way, adjusting the belt, pulling at the sleeves, checking the wristbands, resetting the cap, rituals that are popular with most players. Then there is the dead giveaway, a player whose uniform is actually dirty, grass stained or covered in dirt or gravel. On the other hand, the player who is not playing and whose uniform cannot be soiled unless he fall downs during the pre-game warmup, is too embarrassed to do the kind of uniform rearrangements pursued by his playing colleagues. What need has he to adjust his uniform when in fact his uniform is irrelevant to the activity of the day? He may make a subtle pass at his jersey now and then, perhaps even the occasional cap replacement. He may spit on his shoes for theatrical effect but he knows. He's not playing.

The look on a player's face is also indicative of his playing status. It is, however, difficult to generalize. Some players seem inordinately cheerful, team players who prefer to be so recognized when their real motive is relief at not having to embarrass themselves out on the field. Others are bored, some beyond belief, apathetic to the progress of his team on the field. They are moody. They consider themselves starters, and in fact many of them often are, and when they sit, they are obvious in their displeasure. Some sit stony faced and pained throughout the game, apparently unwilling to pay any attention to its progress. Others will take more dramatic action, including leaving the bench to sit in the stands, as several former Dukes did at one time or another over the years, loudly disputing every call by the umpire, taking a nap, leaving the park entirely, or, in more extreme cases, sitting on the bench and eventually changing in his civilian clothes.

In a recreational league, however, most players riding the pine have expectations that they will play sooner or later. Whether the player on the bench cannot hit a straight pitch with a canoe paddle and a compass is basically irrelevant. He thinks he will play. In the meantime, while he waits, he may keep score, which is the usually the duty of the least hopeless of bench warmers, provided of course that the guy knows how to keep score, he may be asked to coach first or third base where he is obligated to dispense orders to base runners who are not paying attention. Or he may, with the sun on his face and the thought of actually playing close to being gone, simply ride the pine for the pleasure of it, which can be readily acknowledged and understood.

Aside from attempting to ensure that most, if not all available players get an opportunity to play in the game, which at times may seem an unattainable objective, there was always the problem of drawing up the lineup. Hardly a baseball game goes by without some manager somewhere agonizing over deciding where to play everybody. Should he pencil someone named Baxter at second and bat him seventh or play Jones and bat him fifth? Sure, Baxter could field but couldn't hit while Jones could hit but couldn't field. On the other hand, he could play Fredericks. He can't field or hit but at least he pays attention to the base coaches. Then there is the question of the identity of the pitcher. Who's on first indeed? Abbot and Costello couldn't explain it so how could some befuddled manager. Finally, there is that fundamental question of deciding who plays and who was going to sit. Such questions have baffled managers, players and fans since that Doubleday guy claimed to have invented the game.

Remember the late Billy Martin? The guy was a genius between the baselines, a Machiavelli armed with a felt pen and a perpetually pugnacious attitude. He was a field Einstein who knew how to get the best out of his players even though they might have wanted to beat the hell out of him. He won a pennant in every port, most famously as a Yankee manager a least five times and maybe six if he hadn't been out driving on the New Jersey Turnpike one Christmas holiday night. He was man who apparently did not know how to lose. How did he do it? An expertise finely honed by years of patient observation and experience? A well developed sense of the hunch? A scientist approaches with yards of data, now called analytics, crammed in his back pocket like chewing tobacco? Was he a sorcerer? How about blind luck born of desperation. I recall that during the heat of the 1977 American League East pennant race, Martin had Reggie Jackson, his temperamental right fielder and full time nemesis, pick the starting lineup out of a baseball cap belonging to one of pitcher Ron Guidry's kids. The team, who had been in a prolonged slump, went on to win eight straight games with a lineup crafted out of total chance.

The baseball manager is unique among those who are responsible for directing the on field fortunes of a sporting team. In the first place, those with similar duties in other sports are called upon to coach rather than manage, a distinction which, at least according to the dictionary, suggests that a manger only directs while a coach instructs and directs. That would seem to be an accurate assessment, particularly since a baseball manager often employs coaches, most of whom instruct players on one specific area of endeavour, like pitching or hitting, when they were not spitting tobacco juice on their shoes or making ridiculous hand gestures to players on the field. And while most other sports teams do feature assistant coaches, offensive coordinators and the like, suggesting that the head man had some sort of overall management role, only baseball teams choose to employ the appellation of manager.

Another characteristic singular to the baseball manager is the tradition of wearing, more or less, a player's uniform when in pursuit of his duties during a game. Although I don't know anything about the origins of this practice, it is so ingrained in the fabric of the game that any alternate would seem unthinkable. Not that alternatives hadn't been tried. John McGraw, legendary manager of the New York Giants, used to preside over his team wearing a three piece herringbone suit and a black homburg hat. Try that fashion statement today and there would be laughter and then confusion from players, umpires and fans. With respect to other major sports, the obverse of this peculiar fascination with on field attire is equally absurd. Picture Bill Belichick, coach of the New England Patriots, prowling the sidelines in shoulder pads and a helmet. How about coach Nick Nurse of the Toronto Raptors leaping up and down from the bench in baggy shorts and brightly coloured jerseys? Or coach Mike Babcock standing behind the Toronto Maple Leafs in a pair of CCM Tacks?

In addition to these superficial curiosities, the baseball manager is alone, probably more than any others, in exercising his responsibilities. Since baseball is a deliberate, if not cerebrate game with a pace to match, a manger's decisions are easily criticized. Hockey and basketball are too fast and players' performances too interrelated to assign blame to the coach alone. Football may be similar to baseball in its calculated approach to the game but then again, a football coach is surrounded by an army of coordinators, assistants and advisors that each decision seems almost corporate in nature, like there had to be a board meeting before any decision could be made. But a baseball manager, for the most part, is alone in his thoughts, and alone in accepting blame for blunders. Maybe that explains why baseball, probably more than any other sport, occasionally attracts people for whom sanity may be a questionable luxury. Casey Stengel, who guided the New York Yankees to ten American League pennants in twelve years, never made much sense and was celebrated for it. To further support this view of the baseball manager as a person on the edge of lunacy, consider how many coaches in any other sport are regularly ejected from games for kicking dirt on a referee's shoes or throwing equipment into the stands.

Aside from his decisions during a game, which may be mysteries in themselves, as noted earlier, a baseball manager must also decide who is playing where. At first thought, this may not appear to be much of a problem. Most teams, at least in professional leagues, have set starting lineups and established pitching rotations. On the other hand, many major league managers platoon players, depending on who is pitching when. On a recreational team, however, a manger's fate may sometimes be almost cruel. Not only must he construct a lineup that can actually win the game but he must also try to ensure that as many players as possible play as often as they can. This is often not easy and some managers ignore that ambition entirely, preferring to avoid the quandary by only playing their best players at all times. I have been on such teams, even when I have been the so-called manager, having been compelled to take that approach by players who demand to play all the time or not at all. As I have opined occasionally, baseball can become an existential circumstance from which there is no escape but for the shelter of winning. Maybe.

The 1989 season saw the Red Eyes solidify their status as a genuine Ottawa Baseball League dynasty by winning their third championship in the past four years. By then, they had compiled the best record in league history, undeniably demonstrating that they were the best team in league history. The team easily provided the best evidence of their dominance. They had a record team batting average of .345. They scored 247 runs, an average of almost ten runs a game. No other team in the league scored more than 190 runs. They lost only six games of the 34 regular season and playoff games they played. In fact, the only game the Red Eyes lost in the 1989 playoffs was 5-4 to the humble Dukes.

# EVERYTHING CHANGED

O ther league developments in 1989 included the ascension of former former Sun Devil pitcher Jim Dean to league commissioner, a position he would hold for more than a decade, during which time he built the league into the largest of its kind in the country. He also introduced the league to the efficiency of a league hot-line and then the internet, significantly improving the administration of the league. Ironically enough, the Sun Devils, who along with the Dukes formed the basis for the establishment of the league almost a decade before, dropped out of the league for a year, only to re-emerge the next year in a dramatically expanded league.

That expanded league was now to be called the National Capital Baseball League (NCBL), an appellation that remained unchanged from 1990 to 2018, its 37th season. Even before that season began, there were a number of developments. The Senior Interprovincial Baseball League, who had played an interlocking schedule with the Ottawa Baseball League (OBL) in 1989, joined the OBL, resulting in the league name change and increasing the number of teams to seventeen. The number of franchises were slated to grow again before the schedule would start in May. While two teams, the Fanatics and the Astros, the latter one of the 1982 founding teams, folded, they were replaced by the Golden Seals and Kanata Junior Selects. The final pre-season consideration was the creation of another new division, introduced to attract the more recreational player, for whom the original Ottawa Recreational Baseball league was founded by my brother John and for whom the new division was named. Five teams, including three original franchises, the Dukes, the Sweat Sox and the returning Sun Devils, as well as two entirely new teams, the Mustangs and the Double Blues, the latter organized by four well known Ottawa sportswriters, namely Tim Baines, Don Brennan, Bruce Garrioch, and Wayne Scanlan. There were now 23 teams formulated in two tiers and four divisions.

With the dramatic expansion of the league, there was an understandable increase in the number of administrative requirements relevant to the management of a league that now had 23 teams and maybe 250 players. Jim Dean was presumed to be working four to five hours a day at his unpaid position as league commissioner, overseeing all aspects of league operation. Before the league opener, there was the running of the coaching and hitting clinics given by former major league ballplayer Doug Frobel; advertising for new teams and new players; the purchase of equipment, particularly baseballs; the printing of score sheets, lineup cards, and banquet tickets; obtaining permits for the fields and arranging the schedules. During the season, there was a myriad of other duties: updating the league answering machine, checking the fields on game days, overseeing the umpires and the Discipline Committee, and arranging for the trophies and the league banquet. Of course, as much as Jim Dean's efforts were laudatory, if not extraordinary, he had help. People like umpire-in-chief Marcel Nichols, former league President Bruce Stockfish, and the divisional conveners; Dan McKean, John Kohli, Kevin Levya, Randy Fix, the league's first commissioner John Robertson, and former SIBL President Shane Alexander. Overall, it was an impressive achievement by all involved, particularly Mr. Dean.

Aside from managing the team on the field and continuing to publish league as well as team magazines with my brother John, 1990 being the last time John and I would produce a league magazine before others would take over for a couple of years before the entire enterprise would fold. I would occasionally accompany John, who continued to represent the team, to the league meetings, often confusing, calamitous affairs during which the 23 team representatives would discuss league business, argue about league rulings and occasionally compete with each other institutionally. The meetings often exhibited the absurd discourse often heard in the House of Commons although the participants in the NCBL get togethers seldom wore business suits.

With so many teams now in the league, it was difficult to report comprehensively on season results. Several years previously, John and to some extent myself pretty well knew every team and every player in the league. For the first few years of the Ottawa Recreational Baseball League, teams were generally comprised of friends, friends of friends and guys from work. In addition, teams stayed together, at least until players either moved away, moved to a better team or grow weary of embarrassing themselves on the field. But with the league expanding to eleven teams, then to twelve teams and then to 23 teams, the competition become unarguably more keen, precipitating the need to recruit better players and unfortunately dropping less proficient players, directly or indirectly.

John and I were now assembling the league magazine from commentaries provided by the individual teams. So when we reported on the championships won by the prodigal Sun Devils of the Robertson Division of the recreational tier, and the previous champion Ottawa Nepean Canadians of the competitive tier of the league, we were depending on reports from the individual teams engaged in the playoff games. Since our initial purpose in producing a team magazine was intended for our own literary edification, we hardly thought that applied to the league more generally. It was a curious development. Four years before, we were able to publish a magazine in which we supplied individual biographies on maybe 120 players. In 1990, with well more than twice the number of guys playing, we would be lucky to know enough about twenty percent of the league's players to write anything about them. The 1990 edition was our fifth annual league publication and our last. We did, however, continue to distribute a team magazine.

The title of the cover and lead article of the Duke edition of *Baseball Ottawa* was not surprisingly borrowed from the Michael J. Fox film, *Back to the Future*. With the continued expansion of the league and the creation of a recreational division within the league, it seemed appropriate, at least at the time, to recall the history of the league and its successors. Of the six teams that had formed the confederation called the Ottawa Recreational Baseball League, four of them, the Dukes, the Sun Devils, the Sweat Sox and the Red Eyes, had survived the nine years since the league was established in 1982 although it was often noted that an extensively retooled Sun Devil team dropped out for a year before returning with most of the original team intact while the Sweat Sox pretty well did the same thing without leaving the league. Prior to the opening of the 1990 season, both the Astros and the Swingers folded, with members of the Astros, particularly the Pritchard boys, joining other teams while the Swingers combined with elements of the old Canadians to form the Pirates. That left the Red Eyes and the Dukes, the former, the three time league champions and the best team that the league had to offer since its inception, gradually rebuilt while the latter split into two separate teams, one in the Nicholas Division of the so-called competitive part of the newly restructured NCBL and the other, my team, in the newly constituted recreational division, the Robertson Division.

Both Dukes teams had their troubles putting together rosters for the 1990 opener. The competitive team was to be manned by the younger and supposedly more competitive members of the 1989 team while the other Duke team was to be made up with veteran Dukes who were more than eager to start playing regularly again. With two weeks left before the start of the new season, the young Dukes had no money, no management and not enough players. Then Steve Williams, an original Duke, decided to throw his lot in with the young Dukes, which was not surprising since he often appeared to have more in common with the college kids of the young Dukes than with the older Dukes, aside from the fact that he owned a car. For reasons unknown, Mr. Williams then took on the task of organizing the team. For a while, that task seemed overwhelming. Of the 1989 Dukes, only six players, including himself, would be joining the new team. Of the other thirteen from 1989, six would be going to the Duke team in the so-called recreational division, four of whom were players on the original 1982 team, while the remaining seven chose to retire. Williams, using the seemingly endless list of free agents compiled by league president Dean, managed to get a team together. The veteran Dukes, which eventually were to remain the original Duke team that still plays in Tier III of the current NCBL, were able to cobble together a team, the six players from debris of last year's team, including John and I, a brother-in-law, a castoff from the Red Eyes, and two armed forces vets named Cal and Don who managed to play four games between them. As eminent as this group was, it was a team of only ten players, clearly not enough, which quickly became apparent when we had to play the second game with only eight players.

In quick moves that were indicative of something approaching panic, we managed to attract two excellent recruits: Mike Malette was likely the best catcher the team had up until that point and local liquor entrepreneur and renown bon vivant Dave Taylor, who immediately proved himself the best new Duke player since Dick Bondy arrived in 1986. But the future was not looking that bright. Three players, including the two army vets and a kid named Brent, all left the team after a couple of games. Fortunately, they were replaced by Malcolm Larabie who seemed to furnish the Dukes with his pitching and hitting talents every second year since he arrived in 1985, and a fastball player with the unlikely alias of Tom Zanetti who waited until the next season to reveal his true identity. The impersonation was necessary because of the league's rules requiring that team's rosters to be finalized by a certain date. So Mr. Zanetti's name appeared on the 1990 Duke roster, a provisional decision that might come in handy if the need arose. Well, the need did arise and Don Hodge, no longer needing to impersonate Tom Zanetti, later went on to become a Duke legend after fourteen seasons.

Despite the customary hilarity of some games in which the Dukes made multiple errors, the more mature Duke team performed surprisingly well. It managed to win nine and tie one game of the sixteen games it played but lost in a hard fought three game semi-final playoff to the Double Blues, that team of journalists and television personalities, who then went out in three straight to the champions, the resurrected Sun Devils. The Dukes hit .300 as a team and easily led the division in runs and run production. They had five players who hit over .300, including myself. Aside from hitting .354, I also led the division in runs batted in, and hit a triple and three doubles in the three playoff games. (Strangely, individual hitting and pitching statistics for the 22 playoff games played by the Dukes between 1984 and 1993 were never compiled. As a result, my triple and my three doubles in that 1990 playoff series never appeared in any statistics or any Duke publication.) I wouldn't hit .300 for another seven years and never produce another triple for the rest of my NCBL career. In addition to myself, several other original Dukes revived their careers during that season, including pitchers Jack Livingstone and Rob Power, not to mention my brother John who, despite a career batting average below the dreaded Mendoza line, hit an astonishing .391.

The next spring, the spring of 1991 that is, the Dukes celebrated the opening of their tenth season in the National Capital Baseball League. The composition of the historic Duke rosters, both in the current year as well as in years previous, both since and even before the formal establishment of the league, had always been a matter of some fascination, if not a strain on a faulty memory. With the addition of one new player in 1991, the number of players who had played for the Dukes, many of whom never actually played for the 1982 or its successors teams but had been around when the team was still in its sandlot stage, had reached 92, the astounding statistic being that only four of that total were still on the team.

As for the 1991 season in general, the team made the playoffs again although they did lose more games than they won during the regular season. They did, however, continue a team tradition by going down in the first round in the playoffs. During that year, it seemed that the performance of practically everybody on the team declined although John Pole, recovered it seemed from certain lamentable habits, came back from a one year sabbatical to lead the team in hitting. There were still, however, a couple of spectacularly unfortunate Duke failures that resonated well into frequent post-season discussion, particularly at the league banquet, now being held in a community centre in the south end. There was frequent reference during that event that it was probably inevitable that a team as familiar with defeat as the Dukes would reach a low-water mark of sorts when, for the first time in their besotted history they were held hitless in a 19-0 loss to a team called the Golden Seals. The other significant transgression occurred in a playoff game when they managed to parlay an apparent strikeout into a past ball that eventually cleared the bases and thereby gave away the game. As for me, I hit a pedestrian .268 for the season although I did manage two more extra base hits in the playoffs. And by the way, longtime Duke nemesis the Sun Devils won its second of three consecutive divisional championships by winning every regular season and playoff game it played in 1991. The undefeated season may still be a league record.

The Dukes of 1992 proved to be as uneventful as they were during the previous year. On the other hand, they were no different than most of the teams that had preceded them in Duke history. As mysterious and frustrating as an instruction manual accompanying a new laptop, the various Duke teams over the years have usually seemed less than the sum of their parts. It had always been difficult to explain those teams, and the 1992 Dukes were really no different. They somehow managed to turn good hitting, often excellent pitching and barely passable fielding into a recipe for mediocrity. There is a certain mystifying logic that eludes easy explanation but such were the Dukes in 1992. Hard to figure no matter which way one looked at it. So the Dukes fell in the first round of the playoffs, this time to the Neptune Bandits, a new team in the league in 1992 with a strange name and a lot of familiar faces. The only noteworthy event in that playoff was the inexplicable attempt by the Dukes' regular catcher, long known for curious habits and a charmingly tough girlfriend, to steal home. He is thrown out by twenty feet. He then retired to the bench laughably uncontrollably. Spotting the residue of a powdery substance on his upper lip, an innocent teammate asked, "Who brought the donuts?" a memorable Duke quote.

In their eleven year history, this was sixth time and the fourth in succession, that the Dukes had failed to advance beyond the first round of the playoffs, the exception being the 1986 team, which managed to make the semi-finals. Only five members of that team remained to remember the 1986 team which, until an entirely different team won a tier championship more than twenty years later, was the best one in Duke history. The Dukes did improve markedly in 1992, recording a 10-5-3 record, an obvious improvement over their 7-8-3 record of the previous year. Dukes pitching, long a strength of the team since the early days of the league when Rob Power was dominating hitters, remained steady even though Mr. Power, who was known for an attractive wife and attendance at every Super Bowl, had moved to Calgary. In 1992, the staff was led by rookie Brent Bradley, who allowed only five earned runs in winning all five of his starts during the regular season. In addition, the team had three other competent pitchers, veterans Malcolm Larabie, Jack Livingstone, and former phenom John Pole, not to mention myself who picked the win in the only pitching assignment of my Duke career up to that point. It had been a special occasion, my battery mate for the game being my brother John who was retiring after the season.

As a ballpayer, John left a lot to be desired. He couldn't hit with any great authority although he eventually became an accomplished bunter in the later stages of his career, such as it was. He wasn't much of a fielder either although he was serviceable enough, alternating between ensuring that the difficult play looked difficult and the easy play looked like a highlight film. He even insisted on wearing uniform number thirteen, an unfortunate inference until Alex Rodriquez started wearing the number. Most of the veteran players on the Dukes as well as players on other original teams in the National Capital Baseball League were well aware of John's place in, if not his importance to the league. Even John, who passed away several years ago, would have been surprised, if not astounded by today's National Capital Baseball League and its 37 teams. It was all John's call all the way in those days, not just for the team but the league as well: the organization, the budget, the telephone calls (no e-mails then), the written schedules, up all night with the league statistics, which were gleaned from team score sheets, many of which were difficult to decipher, ensuring that the league was provided with umpires, that each team had enough baseballs and the team was appropriately equipped, mainly wooden bats in the early days, then aluminum and then back to wooden bats a couple of years ago. Even though John was occasionally and haphazardly assisted by the team representatives, not to mention my own efforts to help out, it was pretty well John's show in those days. Without John, there would have not been a team or a league. It was that simple.

Although John sought to found the league and the team in order to play baseball, and indeed John was the team's regular catcher that first year, he consistently gave up his own playing time for others. A quick perusal of the statistics have shown that John consistently received less playing time than any anyone else on the team, including several who appeared to have great difficulty staying awake during most of the games. And still, despite such obvious sacrifices, John, and myself many years later, also had to countenance the complaints of those who had the nerve to protest their lack of playing time even though their contributions to the team on the field were no greater than either of ours. John and I also consistently lost money on the team, often using our own money for a needed piece of equipment and sometimes a shortage in the league fee. In addition, he and I invested our own time and money in producing a team, and for a time a league magazine. In fact, so extreme was my own obsession that I continued to publish a team magazine for almost another twenty years even though, certainly in my last decade or so of being on a Duke roster, I played little, if at all, my own ability as a player judged by the team as wanting. There was little point in searching for a fitting coda to John's career as a Duke. Although he stayed associated with the team, even playing the occasional game when we were on the edge of a forfeit, it was for years strange playing on the team without him.

John played his last game for the team he founded almost twenty years ago.

# THE CONTINUUM OF STYLE

In the team magazine celebrating the accomplishments, so to speak, of the 1991 Dukes, I was featured in a photograph holding a bat while dressed in a tuxedo. The irony of that picture introduced an article on the fashion consciousness of baseball players since Abner Doubleday showed up to invent baseball in a farmers field in upstate New York presumably wearing an oversized but matching flannel shirt and trouser outfit akin to a military uniform, wool knee socks, spiked leather shoes and a cap that would not have looked out of place in the Crimean War.

I began that article by recalling my exhilaration with first seeing my eternal hero Mickey Mantle of the New York Yankees on television. It was some summer Saturday afternoon in the late 1950's. I was eight or nine years old. My father, having recently installed a television antenna, was enthusiastically introducing the family to the delights of American broadcasting. He was busily flipping through the available channels, after all he had considerable reason to be proud, having recently added three U.S. channels to the two Canadian ones with which we were previously acquainted. Mickey appeared on the twelve inch, black and white screen. I immediately went into some sort of shock, my familiarity with my first real boyhood hero having been previously limited to baseball cards and the exotica of New York city radio.

It was Mantle alright, two inches high on the television screen but still Mantle. While it may have taken me several minutes to get my bearings, my senses having been separated from the rest of me by some sort of undefined rapture, I was able to persuade my quizzical father to leave the baseball game on rather than switch the channel for the hundredth time in the last fifteen minutes. I settled in to watch Mickey, my face maybe a foot from the screen. My mother, who had been watching my father fiddle with the television, yelled at me for potentially ruining my eyes. Mantle was approaching the plate with that imperial stride of his, head down, seemingly imperious to the significance of the moment. I was going to see Mickey Mantle hit. He stepped in, batting lefthanded, took a few practice swings, and waited, bat cocked high over his head, slight crouch, hands held in close to his body. I waited as well.

I cannot now recall the events that unfolded before me that afternoon on that black and white television screen. While Mantle definitely did not hit a home run, for I would have remembered that, I cannot say, with any sort of certainty, whether he struck out, which he did with frequency and flourish, grounded out uneventfully, popped out to the catcher, hit a long flyball to the wrong part of Yankee Stadium, or lined a double over first. I cannot say. All I can remember with any accuracy is his uniform, the way he tugged at it and casually rearranged the placement of his batting helmet after every pitch. I had no explanation of my fascination with the way Mickey Mantle was dressed. Not that it was particularly important but it stood out somehow. His uniform.

Baseball uniforms, like those of most sports I suppose, have always been a significant element of the experience of the sport, as if they circumscribed the events and times in which the players that wore them performed. Take Mantle that day I first saw him on television, on that black and white screen. As I was later to discover after reading an otherwise tiresome volume on the history of the lordly New York Yankees, Mickey was wearing an ajax white uniform with royal blue lettering. It was loose fitting, baggy in the way most attire was in the 1950s, a heavy flannel that hung on some players like an unused sail on a boat under anchor. His cleats were uniform black, unadorned with stripes or the manufacturer's name, plain, low cut and completely forgettable. Like most, if not all, players, Mantle wore his sock stirrups high, showing a thin strip of stirrup, his pants pulled up to a spot well past the ankle to accommodate plenty of stirrup strip. Interestingly enough, the stirrup was pretty well the only frivolous part of Mantle's costume, its origins being identification, now unnecessary, rather than function.

In this context, the stirrup was first worn by teams in the late nineteenth century to identify themselves. Hence, the origins of team monikers like the Red Sox, the White Sox, and the Red Stockings (a.k.a. Legs). Since most teams wore the same uniforms, the ability to construct an array of different uniforms limited by economics, they were generally identified by the colour of their socks, a practicality which necessitated the development of the stirrup, the principal means of telling one team from another on the field. Not that such differentiation was actually necessary for the very structure of the game of baseball as a game, unlike basketball, football or hockey for example, does not require that a great deal of attention be paid to sorting out which player plays on which team. It was fairly obvious. But they did it anyway. One could suppose that fans might get upset if an effort wasn't made to ensure that they knew which team was at bat and which team was in the field.

Historically, there have been differences in the way baseball players wore the humble stirrup. Fifty or sixty years ago, players tried to show as little stirrup as they could, usually pulling them and their pant legs up high to leave only a thin strip of material showing, thereby exposing their spectacular calf muscles to presumably appreciative fans. In fact, there was the story of one enterprising player attempted to do away with stirrups entirely by painting a line in the appropriate place on the white socks players usually wear under the stirrup. Than, more thirty years ago, players began wearing their stirrups and pants as low as they could go, thereby showing off the top of their stirrups rather the thin strip of material. In any event, the stirrup is now a matter of individual taste and is littler noticed, unless of course you wanted to wear them over your ears.

Above the stirrup were the pants, pinstriped in the case of the Yankees, an elegance of design that makes a lot of other teams, the tasteless oranges and yellows of the pants of teams like Baltimore, Pittsburg and San Diego or the shorts worn by the Chicago White Sox in the late 1970s, look like circus clowns. In addition, ball players' uniforms used to be extremely loose fitting, requiring about as much material you would need for a small tent. They were cotton flannel and were uncomfortable, particularly in warm weather. They had belt loops, a convenience which allowed players to wear black leather belts with individual belt buckles. The shirt, or blouse as they were once called, was also baggy. They were short sleeved, usually front buttoned although not always buttoned, and, tucked in the pants, although sometimes baggy enough to hang over the belt in large folds. The team insignia or name was emblazoned on the front of the shirt, or jersey as they eventually came to be called.

A short detour here. Traditionally, and to this day, home uniforms feature the team's insignia or nickname while away uniforms indicate the name of the city that the team represents. No one knows why this was the case although one could speculate that this was for the benefit of feeble minded fans who could not figure out, for example, that the Yankees came from New York rather than Lincoln, Nebraska. In any event, uniform jerseys in the early days carried no identifiable marks, no numbers, no names, no badges, and no commemorative appellations of any sorts. Sometime in the 1920s, numbers were added while names started to appear in the 1970s. Modern players do not burden themselves with the commercial indignities of tennis, soccer or European hockey players, who have developed an affinity for badges, labels or tags advertising one thing or another.

Nonetheless, the basic uniform has not really changed in any substantive way in the past fifty or sixty years. There are much tighter it seems than they used to be, owing more one can suppose to the modern player's vanity than advances in uniform design or fabrics. Some have belts, some don't. They are made of more resilient materials, lighter and more durable. Most have the player's name embroidered on the back, a detail that would have been sacrilegious in the old days. They are generally more colourful, although experiments like the White Sox uniforms of the mid-1970s, which came with shorts and floppy collars, are simply indicative of the risk of an occasional lapse.

One has to admit, regardless of changes in uniform design and the like, that the modern player appears to be a fairly different character than his antecedents of a thousand years ago. There is little doubt that he is bigger, faster, stronger and in much better physical condition, a development that would surely disqualify Babe Ruth from even making a major league team, let alone revolutionizing the game as they knew it then. The modern uniform accentuates a player's physique while old fashion uniforms hide it. If Lou Gehrig were alive today, he'd looked great, much better than he did in the 1920s when he was hitting .350 wearing those baggy flannels. On the other hand, Babe Ruth would probably look worse, his beer belly and ballerina legs emphasized by the form fitting modern uniform.

# INNINGS

Aside from the basic outfit, the modern baseball player affects a number of accessories to which his predecessors did not have access. The most obvious of these is the batting glove, a convenience, maybe even a fashion statement, that was first worn by Boston Red Sox first baseman Ken "The Hawk" Harrelson back in the late 60s. Harrelson, who was somewhat of a dandy anyway, having affected Nehri jackets and beads when most of his teammates were still wearing madras jackets and chinos, begin wearing a golf glove because, as he pointed out to an inquisitive reporter at the time, he was in a slump and "it looks kind of cool". Within two or three years, more than half of the players in the major leagues were wearing batting gloves to the plate. A lot of them started wearing batting gloves in the field as well. Today, it is difficult to find a major league player who doesn't wear a batting glove at the plate. In fact, a majority wear a glove on both hands rather than on the lower hand on the bat, which was the choice of the pioneers of this development. Wearing of batting gloves may have, however, contributed to the glacial pace of baseball game these days as a number of players seem to adjust their batting gloves after every pitch, a habit that seems to have increased over the years. The popularity of the batting glove is so manifest that announcers often make a point of commenting on any player that does not wear them, so rare is the player who comes to the plate holding a bat with his bare hands. Evan Gattis of the World Champion of 2017 Houston Astros is a recent example.

Finally, there is the modern player's penchant for wearing other accessories, like wrist bands and necklaces, worn it seems more like decorations or fashion statements than any consideration of function. Regarding wrist bands, some players like to wear several wrist bands on each arm, making players look like they are about to pour steel rather than swing at a curve ball. I recall going to Montreal Expo games back in the 1970s and being horribly impressed by the fashion sense of Expo Rodney "Wrist Band" Scott who had the habit of wearing at least three wrist bands on each arm. Even if he struck out twice and couldn't get a ball out of the infield, he had already made his contribution to the game by coming to it well dressed. What more could a fan ask?

I would estimate that in almost sixty years of playing recreational baseball, having played for maybe twenty teams, including more than twenty five years for one team, I must have worn at least that many different uniforms. For the Dukes, I wore at least seven different uniforms, ranging from cheap blue t-shirts, several varieties of blue and white uniforms, black jerseys with white pants, tomato red jerseys with the same white pants, grey/blue uniforms, and for maybe ten years or so pinstripe uniforms with a stylized "D" on the left side of the chest. For the last few years of my association with the Dukes, the team wore white uniforms with dark piping and the team name "Dukes" on the front and player numbers on the back in a fashionable teal colour. Unfortunately, my status over the last three years of my career with the team apparently did not qualify me to be issued a uniform, leaving me to wear old baseball pants and a plain t-shirt, just like I did in those days before I was first given my first uniform in little league back in 1960.

Any musings regarding the place of baseball uniforms in the development of the game may lead to a reference to the importance of the sponsor to any recreational baseball league and its teams. During my experience with little league baseball, one of my more persistent recollections involved the various team sponsors, an arcane though I suspect a widespread phenomenon. Anybody who played little league may occasionally have had similar ruminations. In the league I played in, or at least attempted to play in, there were a number of local enterprises, their civic duty presumably discharged by acts of such charity, who could be counted on every year to fork out whatever it cost to outfit fifteen ten to twelve year olds in baseball uniforms which, more often or not, looked like they had been designed by someone with a profound lack of fashion taste. Not that it mattered a great deal. After all, our parents had only paid a dollar for us to join a team.

Little league baseball was curious that way. Pee wee hockey, not to mention Pop Warner football, seemed to be perpetually without such obvious support, sporting names like Black Hawks, Maroons, Colts and Bears while their baseball colleagues pursued their fates with names like Hub Hardware, P.C. Lemaire Plumbing, MacDermott's, Johnson's Drugs, Fraser Sports and Helen's Taxi emblazoned on their jerseys. No one could offer a satisfactory explanation of this apparent discrepancy in behaviour

# INNINGS

although I have always suspected that somewhere there was and still is a nameless sports bureaucrat who established guidelines about naming sports teams. Not that it really mattered to anyone. I mean, we all were quite capable of playing poorly regardless of whether the monikers on our sweaters made reference to a member of the animal kingdom or a local grocery store.

My first baseball team was called Johnson's Drug, an appropriate name given the condition of our coach's stomach much of the time. Like a lot of little leaguers, we could be woefully inept at times, almost fatalistically inefficient, to a point that sometimes precipitated the perception that we were unfamiliar with the game. We wore forest green uniforms with Johnson's Drug displayed prominently on our chest. We never knew how this venerable pharmacy came to sponsor a little league baseball team. As far as I knew, the owner, who supposedly looked like a cross between Cardinal Richelieu and Marcus Welby, never came to a game, never showed up at the banquet and had no interest whatsoever in the machinations of baseball, little league or otherwise. Why would such an individual, who scared the hell out of us every time we showed up at the candy counter with a nickel, want to sponsor a ball team? Civic pride? Hardly likely since we were generally an embarrassment to ourselves, let alone the city. Tax shelter? Maybe but we were ten, eleven and twelve years old and wouldn't know a tax dodge from a fungo bat. In cynical shorthand, the man had no angle that we could speak of. We never did figure out the basis for Mr. Johnson's philanthropy even though a decade or so of befuddled little leaguers had had the opportunity to contemplate the question while they were booting ground balls dressed in those forest green uniforms.

Back to the future of middle age and the hundreds, if not thousands of recreational baseball teams reliving past glories on weekends and every weekday evening. Many of these teams, no matter how good or how bad, seem to have sponsors, the names of bars, restaurants, plumbing companies, or sporting good stores stencilled on their jerseys with varying degrees of flourish. In fact, the aforementioned enterprises are usually among the most likely to sponsor recreational sporting endeavours, including baseball. While the reasons for their generosity can never be known, particularly among those of us who regard cynicism as a virtue, there are number of obvious motivations who can be reasonably considered.

First of all, let's take the most popular types of sponsor, bars and restaurants. The motivation here seems obvious enough. For a small outlay of cash, the amount usually dependent on the sponsored team's ability to plead its case, the bar or restaurant gets a helluva lot of free advertising. The underwritten team, no matter how good or how mediocre, even if it is playing bush league slow pitch in the middle of the night in a parking lot, supplies the sponsor with some sort of profile, even if it is minimal. In addition, even if the so-called free advertising fails to increase the sponsor's prospects in any measurable way, he can reasonably expect that the team to which he has extended all this largess will at least frequent his place of business. That is why, for example, bars or restaurants are often enthusiastic about sponsoring a mixed team, reasoning that having a group of men and women in baseball/softball teams frequenting their place is better than serving drafts to a group of sullen men whose only interest in baseball is apathy. Speaking of apathy, there may be some sort of satisfaction, however difficult it may be to define, to be gained from having your name all over somebody's uniform. It has always been good enough for Calvin Klein or Ralph Lauren, hasn't it?

The most persuasive element of any pitch you may make for a sponsorship is the fact that you are either employed by the enterprise or have spent a considerable amount of time cultivating its services. It is much easier, for example, to interest a company in a sponsorship if you or, better still, if you and several of your teammates work there. A less preferable though less viable alternative involves a bar or restaurant where you and your friends spend a lot of time. Perhaps this explains why bars and restaurants are much more popular choices for sponsors. After all, one seldom spends much time hanging around appliance or hardware stores. Over the years, there has been an ebb and flow to the level of National Capital Baseball League when it came to team sponsorship. For at least half of the over twenty years I was involved in the management of the Dukes, the team had a sponsor. Its first sponsor, and the bar which gave the team's original name, was actually a gathering place for soccer or rugby players. It was an oversight that was corrected after two years when the owner became aware that the Dukes were actually a baseball team. Over the next twenty years or so, the Dukes were sponsored by a variety of bars, restaurants and at least one retail outlet, places with names like the

# INNINGS

Schadillac Saloon, the Great Lakes Brewery, Bumpers Cafe, the Sunnyside Sports Club, the Ottawa Sports Gallery, Mexicali Rosa's and, for a brief time in 2004, Casey's Grill, individual largess which invariably lasted no more than a season even though the names sometimes remained inscribed on the uniforms until the team changed those uniforms.

# LOST IN THE 1990S

Once again, in an almost tiresome indication of its history, change was inevitable for the Dukes of 1993. Aside from getting along without the now retired league and team founder John Robertson, the most important adjustment for the Dukes would be the requirement to compete at an appreciably higher level in 1993. The league, in a burst of wisdom that some had argued was overdue, would be realigned into three rather than previous two two tiers, each tier accommodating progressively competitive teams. The Dukes, occupants of the sometimes ironically named recreational division for the previous four years, would join the Sun Devils, the Southpaw Production Braumeisters, the Mustangs and the Neptune Palace Bandits in moving up to the newly established Nicholas and Yanis Divisions, which together came to be known, rather glamorously, as Tier II. Several other teams would move from the Wallace and Jordan Divisions, which had been colloquially known as the competitive division, to join the four previously noted aspirants. A couple of new entrants and the National Capital Baseball League would now have 32 teams playing in three separate tiers and six divisions, the whole structure now featuring maybe 500 players playing 450 regular season games. The realignment went ahead without apparent difficulty, another testament to the organizational acumen of the soon to be retiring league president Jim Dean. It was quite an achievement for a league that a little more than a decade ago was playing only six teams and holding its meetings at a table in a local tavern.

As for the Dukes, the loss of team manager emeritus John Robertson and my own reluctance to continue to run the team on the field resulted in the emergence of Brian Bradley, entering only his fourth year as a Duke, as the team general/field manager, a decision that predictably he was soon to regret. The team, even though it had lost only five of eighteen games last

# INNINGS

year, had to improve, the requirement to play against better teams making that requirement inevitable. Besides, the team had some holes to fill in any event. Peter Johns, the team's starting shortstop, outfielder Greg Tullock and utility man Steve Courtland, the latter renown not only for his speed but for his fanciful nickname "Dweeble", were all leaving to form a new venture in the Tier III division. With John gone, at least four of the fifteen spots would be empty. The elder Bradley, who had not planned to play very much himself, suddenly faced the unenviable prospect of attracting new players. In addition, as I was happy to realize, my successor as field manager would now be burdened with the responsibilities of recruiting new players. In this context, with the addition of nine new teams to the league over the last two seasons, the Dukes would have increased competition for new players. On the other hand, with the arrival of the Ottawa Lynx, a Triple A farm team of the Montreal Expos, it could be assumed that enthusiasm for baseball in the city had improved and would likely continue to improve, meaning than more players would want to join the league.

Not unlike previous history, a piece of fortune landed in the laps of Duke management during a league meeting in March. Bradley, John Pole and I happened to be seated near a certain Dave Straznicky of the Giants, a team that appeared to be on the verge of collapse. After some negotiation, during which Bradley promised not to bore any new recruits with stories of his Saturdays nights in the Carleton Place hotel, Straznicky delivered himself and teammate Matt Dewan to the Dukes, both of whom would eventually turn out to be among the team leaders in hits. In addition, eventual team stolen base leader and ex-umpire Chris Gray and former Duke pitcher Tom Wudwud, who won 23 games for the Dukes between 1984 and 1990, were enticed to re-join the team for the 1993 season. On the administrative side, Dave Taylor, his power of persuasion known to every bartender in the city, was busy lining up a new sponsor for the Dukes, the team's first sponsoring benefactor since the Dukes of Somerset in 1982. The newly opened Schadillac Saloon on Murray Street, owned and operated by former Philadelphia Eagle and Queen's University Golden Gael Mike Schad and his brother Andre, were kind enough to supply the team with new uniforms, classy black jerseys, pin stripe pants, and sporty new caps being the most recent fashion statement for a team that used to wear cheap t-shirts, sweatpants and their own baseball caps. As always it seemed, things were looking good for the team, at least for a while.

Although the team eventually made the playoffs, the regular season was a series of peaks and valleys on which one could base a fairly respectable soap opera. We would occasionally play almost impeccable baseball, a 8-0 victory over eventual Tier I champion Expos comes to mind. We could play surprisingly tough baseball, a 7-5 loss to the Rebels was one such example. But, on the other hand, we could play simply terrible baseball, humiliating losses to the Sun Devils, the Yankees, and Braumeisters being offered into evidence. Still, even though the Dukes lost five more games than they won in 1993 and posted a profoundly pedestrian, if not ignoble record of 7-12-2, they still managed to scrap into the playoffs, an eventuality that prompted serious questions about the number of teams that were qualified for the playoffs. The team was disoriented as they were entering those playoffs, stunned by four consecutive losses at the end of the regular season. They looked ready to be simply rolled out of the playoff picture like a piece of old furniture. They would be playing the Rebels, the winners of the division and a team with a legitimate shot at the title. Still, the Dukes looked like they had a chance in a short series, having beaten the Rebels handily in their first meeting and narrowly losing in the second.

They lost a tragically close one in that first playoff game, another one of those Duke struggles that could easily qualify for ascension into the hierarchy of Duke playoff heart breakers, of which history had recorded several. To suggest that the Dukes should have, very possibly would have or quite definitely could have won game one was varying degrees of cliche. After all, they jumped out to a 7-0 lead by the third inning. They had built the lead on the strength of big hits like Dave Taylor's triple, timely hits like Keith Godin's three run flare to left and some aggressive base running. Even so, their lead could have been much higher had they been able to produce more than two runs from several bases loaded situations in the fourth inning, a failure highlighted by my own inability to get a suicide squeeze down from a ball thrown at my head. I cannot recall who gave him the sign for the bunt although everybody denied it after the game. Dave Taylor, running with the pitch, was dead at the plate and something changed. In the home half of that inning, the Rebels scored two runs. It was the start of something bad for the Dukes. In the sixth inning, things really started to hit the skids for the Dukes. It was an inning in which the Dukes make four fielding errors and a 7-2 lead was gone and the Rebels were suddenly leading 8-7. To their credit, the Dukes did not quit. Several walks, a badly played ground ball or two, a double steal, a couple of hits and the Dukes go into the bottom of the seventh inning leading the Rebels 10-8. But their good fortune was not to continue. A walk, three consecutive infield errors, a couple of line drives and the Dukes were done, losing 11-10.

Anti-climax is too flippant a term to characterize the fate of the team in those last two games of those playoffs. They beat the Rebels 8-2 in the next game behind the brilliance of veteran Jack Livingstone on the mound and the spectacular fielding of Dave Taylor at third base, a position that was apparently new to him. Game three, though, was an entirely different matter. Like most seasons, the last Duke loss of 1993 was probably inevitable. Only nine Dukes bothered to show up for a comedy of a game in which the Dukes made a number of errors, produced little offence and were generally listless in losing 9-2. Another season was over, another punch line forgotten.

On paper, and probably by pretty well every other possible standard, there is little doubt that the 1994 edition of the team in which I thought I had invested so much time and effort was the worst in its thirteen year history. The team was almost surrealistically inept, so much so that no one, particularly the players themselves, ever even talked about it. The team managed a winless streak that reached a zenith of nineteen games between May 10 and July 24, their only two victories in the first and last games of the season. A couple of original Dukes, Jack Livingstone and myself, could occasionally and sardonically refer to such previous Duke assemblies as the 1982 team, which won only five out of twenty games, and the 1988 team, which took only six out of twenty seven games. My own musings on the comparisons between the 1994 team and any other Duke team seemed pointless somehow, particularly since the league in which the Dukes played and the teams against which it competed had changed so significantly in those thirteen years. On the other hand, regardless of the relative competitiveness of the team's opponents, two wins is two wins and that is the fewest any Duke team has ever managed.

As expected, as for any disaster, there was an explanation. For the 1994

Duke team, fortunes for that season took a downturn well before the it started. The Bradley brothers, erstwhile team manager Brian and pitcher Brent, announced that they wouldn't be returning. Brian, who sometimes allowed his managerial duties to overwhelm him, had not played much in 1993 and therefore wasn't expected to make much of a difference, at least on the field. On the other hand, the loss of Brent, despite his frequent bursts of curious behaviour, fuelled it was rumoured by something other than Red Bull, would be catastrophic, his .296 batting average and his 7-3 pitching record over the past two seasons gone from the roster. And on top of that, and maybe more importantly, Matt Dewan, a Duke rookie who hit .319 and played a great outfield in 1993, reluctantly left for the Tier I team in Kanata. Three players were gone and the snow hadn't left the ground. In addition, veteran pitcher Tom Wudwud suddenly quit without explanation.

Meanwhile, it had become apparent that most teams in Tier II were improving, some dramatically. Tier I and big league free agents were apparently being signed by Tier II teams at a frantic pace, or said the rumours circulating among team representatives at league meetings in particular. It should be noted that back then, there was no league website to advertise for or attract new players. As always, only rumour, hearsay or scuttlebutt among current league players were the primary methods of communication. Even the open tryouts at the Lynda Lane diamonds had been discontinued. In any event, the Sun Devils, the Expos, eventual Tier II champion the Athletics, the Mustangs, the Braumeisters, were all familiar teams with unfamiliar names on their rosters. All teams seemed to be getting younger and presumably better. And then there were the Dukes. The sole ambition of another barely willing general manager, this time in the person of John Pole, and myself, unfortunately back on the job as field manager after a short hiatus, was to ensure that the Dukes had nine players with which to open the season. Despite our efforts, things didn't look so good. Basketball player and self-professed fastball player Joe Panek, who was an entertaining collection of irritating exuberance, unsolicited advice, and general name calling, was the only new player the team managed to recruit, at least before the season began.

So the team entered the season with only ten players on roster. Then things got worse when Dave Straznicky, who hit over .400 for the Dukes in

# INNINGS

1993, appeared in only the opening game of the season before disappearing into the team history. Over the next several weeks, during which the Dukes were losing their next four games by double digit scores, they managed to sign three new players: pitcher Rob Lorenz, who arrived from the Expos amid less than salutatory circumstances; Yvan Plamondon, a friend of Joe Panek who was signed out of bleachers when only seven Dukes showed up for a game against the Thunder; and the most sardonically prized recruit of all, a bon vivant and street raconteur named Keith Shields who would go on to make quite an impression on a team for whom he would play for the next four seasons. Around the same time, Dave Taylor, who occasionally led the team in hitting, dapper sportswear and hedonistic behaviour over the past three seasons, went on injury reserve for the remainder of the year. In a commentary unlikely to be contradicted by anyone who lived through a season in which the team won only two of twenty one games, pretty well everything went wrong for the Dukes in 1994. Well, maybe almost everything. Duke pitching, almost always a strength, continued a proud tradition by labouring well for a losing enterprise, the core of the staff — Malcolm Larabie, Jack Livingstone and newcomer Rob Lorenz — all pitched well enough to win more than two games.

Larabie in particular deserved much better, winning only one game and losing six but keeping his earned run average at a very respectable 3.65. In the end, Duke pitching was cursed by their inability to strike out every batter they faced. By allowing the opposition to get the bat on the ball, they ran the risk of depending on Duke fielding, always a dubious proposition. The team's abysmal fielding, traditionally a weakness anyway, was amplified by the fact that for the first time in team history, fielding statistics were collected. This was bad news, not only for the team, which made more than a hundred errors, but for at least seven individuals who were so bad that each one of them bungled more than two out of every ten fielding chances they tried to handle. By way of explanation, not excuse, the 1994 Dukes had real trouble establishing a set defence. Aside from catcher Mike Malette and first baseman Dan Hodge, the Dukes were all over the field: seven different guys played second base, seven at third base, six at shortstop and an astounding thirteen different players in the outfield, including at least four who eventually quit the team. No wonder one could conclude. As for me, I played every position but pitcher and catcher, making only seven of the 109 errors the team made. As for the offence, the team hit a dreadful .195, collecting a hundred base hits less than their opposition. They had five regular players who fell below the dreaded Mendoza line of a .200 batting average, including two who were barely above the double Mendoza line. As for me, I managed to hit a pedestrian .268, which amazingly enough was second on the team in hitting, demonstrating the sorry state of the team's offence that season. Perhaps the most fitting epitaph for the 1994 team emerged during the team's last official act for the year. During deliberations to pick the league's trophy winners, it was noted that each appropriate section for the Dukes read simply: "No Candidates".

It was difficult to say anything positive about the 1994 Dukes except that they did, for the most part, retain their usually bemused fatalism about serial losing. Their utterly relaxed attitude toward losing prompted me to evaluate the ancient bromide about it not being about winning or losing but how you played the game. It was fairly obvious to me that the often repeated homily gave comfort to most of my teammates on the 1994 Dukes, whether they realized it or not. In contemplating losing, I concluded that it has a grand tradition in all sports, including baseball where there is a long list of failures. We have long admired the great teams but are captivated by the unlucky ones, the tragic, the star crossed teams whose losses have provided them with identities that elevate them into unintended myth. Although it was more than fifty years ago, I still can recall the 1964 Philadelphia Phillies who lost the National League pennant to St. Louis by one game after losing the last eight games of the season. Of course, there are others, the 1986 Boston Red Sox who lost the World Series because Bill Buckner allowed a ground ball to skitter through his legs in game six. My team, the New York Yankees, losing four consecutive games to lose the 2004 American League championship to the Red Sox, and before that, the 1960 team allowing a light hitting second baseman named Bill Mazeroski to hit a home run in the bottom of the ninth inning in the seventh game to win the series for the Pittsburg Pirates. More recently, the Chicago Cubs took more than a hundred years to finally win a series by beating a team, the Cleveland Indians, who haven't won a title since Harry Truman was President. And there are likely hundreds more, tragic tales, tales of triumph and misfortune, and finally, tales of losing.

# INNINGS

Then there is the truly pathetic, like the Dukes of 1994 one can suppose, when losing is little more than a comedy skit, the entertainment being not in the fact of losing but in the method. Certainly more famed were the 1962 New York Mets, who featured players like Marvelous Marv Throneberry and Choo Choo Coleman, both of whom played the field as if they were wearing hoods over their heads and oven mitts on their hands; teams so bad that they were difficult not to like, if not to admire. Replete with foibles, such teams raise losing to an art form. Hell, people went to see them lose, not to see them possibly win, even the syndrome of the underdog not in play here, it was the losing that kept the fans loyal. The fascination was in the way such teams lost. They just didn't fail to win, they lost, profoundly, undeniably. They were unimpeachable losers. They seldom had hope and when they did, they would conspire to throw the game away, as if winning was a curse from which they sought to escape. How else to explain a team, like the 1994 Dukes for example, that managed to hit less than .200 as a team, a collective decline below the dreaded Mendoza line.

Those 1962 Mets, a team that the 1994 Dukes may have most resembled, were an exception that probably proves the rule. Being on a losing team, no matter how entertaining to spectators with a death wish, is usually not much fun. Players on such teams are sometimes marked for life, forever expectant of the worst, they hope to win but labour for the loss, constantly contemplating its end, not as if it were any kind of slump but some sort of permanent condition from deliverance was a doubtful prospect. As individuals, players react in a number of different but predictable ways to constant losing. As a team, these different reactions can turn a collection of players from a team into a group therapy.

The preferable reaction for a player toiling for a losing team is not take any notice of it, a strategy that is sometimes pursued by many of my teammates on various Duke teams over the years. Such players play as if nothing is amiss, every inning a challenge, regardless of the score. Such players are a manger's delight, making full effort on the field, they are the basis on which the team will turn a losing team around. A variant of this is the player who plays as if he simply cannot believe that the team is actually losing. He regards the score, no matter how often it is repeated, as some sort of fabrication, as if the umpires, the other team, even his own teammates, are all in on some sort of practical joke. There are problems with both of these approaches. Such players, however laudatory their behaviour may seem, are usually disliked by less optimistic teammates, their continually upbeat demeanour annoying to less cheerful players. The latter, on the edge of depression, ceaselessly mimic the theatrics of such players and discuss ways of nailing his shoes to the bench. In summary, such players make other players look bad.

Constant losing has been known to cause psychological dysfunction, the losing having sent many a player, not to mention his manager, entirely off his rocker. They are happy losers, so jaded by losing that they, without embarrassment or intended sarcasm, cheer every triumph, no matter how trivial. Advance on a passed ball, the catch of a lazy pop fly, a routine ground ball to short, a pathetic flare to right, all may ignite the most outrageous of celebrations. Some of these players may cross the line into psychosis, a state in which they may be found taking the field in a diaper. I recall that one of my esteemed colleagues on the 1994 Dukes, in the last the season, taking up his position in right field wearing swim trunks, flip flops and sitting in a deck chair. When chided about it after the game, which was mercifully called when the umpire was told that we had only eight players, the individual only laughed.

The final group of players in such an informal study are those who show definite signs of emotional dislocation. They may sulk, they may get mad, they may get morose, they may refer to suicide as "something to do tonight". Such players are deeply affected by losing, so much so that they find themselves in the deep crevices of either despair or rage, unwilling to make a choice between a gas oven or a small calibre handgun. I personally have only come across one or two such players. One of them, a player who was not much of a player anyway, used to actually come to tears after losing, which could have happened a lot on a team like the Dukes. The other liked to throw equipment around after a defeat. As for the player in swim trunks and flip flops, that was his last inning as a Duke, a career that had lasted only that one season anyway.

For the second time in three years, the Dukes entered the 1995 season with five new players and another new uniform. You didn't have to be genius for prognostication to predict that there would be significant changes for the Dukes in 1995. Any observers, no matter how short of insight, would eventually figure out that any team that won only two games the previous season would be compelled to make changes. After all, no matter how serene the team appeared to be after so disastrous a season, no one could be satisfied with so inauspicious a season. Last in practically every possible category of statistic, the 1994 club would definitely not stand the test of time, regardless of how long that could or would be. However, before the season began, the Dukes were victorious with respect to a number of issues, including in particular avoiding demotion of the Duke franchise to Tier III, which might not have been a bad idea given their two win season in 1994.

Under the unlikely management of long time Duke catcher Mike Malette, the team confounded cynics by attracting two new sponsors, the Great Lake Brewery and Bumpers Cafe on Bank Street, purchasing new bright red uniforms, recruiting a number of new players and surviving the resignations of two incumbent Dukes: Chris Gray and Joe Panek, the latter memorialized by his unique conversational skills, his comic hitting and curious fielding. Regarding new Dukes for 1995, there was Matt Dewan, a Duke rookie in 1993, returning to the team after a season in Tier I, Neil Corriveau arriving from the Mustangs, Alberto Rosario and Santo Vasquez from the Dominican Republic and Ken "Whitey" Watson, who looked like he could have appeared on the cover of an old Beach Boy record. The team would also have the benefit of the full time services of Yvan Plamendon, an extremely useful and versatile player who played only six games in 1994. Sure, there were the failed experiments, a couple of other new players came and went, but overall, despite the predictable doubts, not to mention the odd quibble with the new uniforms, the Dukes entered the season as a better team.

The season started unfortunately with a 8-2 defeat to the Yankees, precipitating a certain dread from those Dukes who had lived through last year's two win season. But any possible despair evaporated over the next two weeks. During that period, the Dukes beat the Lynx, the Braumeisters, and the Thunder, three consecutive victories that ensured that the team would end the 1995 season with a much better record than they managed in 1994. It was heady stuff. With Corriveau and Dewan on permanent patrol in the outfield, the resurgent Shields, whose familiarity with the Triple A Ottawa Lynx was becoming legend, showing a remarkable talent for producing the big hit, the newly arrived Dominicans Rosario and Vasquez, adding muscle to the lineup, and most others looking better than they did last year, the Dukes were suddenly and unexpectedly optimistic. It was presumed to be a strange feeling for most of veteran Dukes.

The season then went on a predictable roller coaster ride through the peaks and valleys of mediocrity. By early July, they were three games over .500 and in the definite hunt for a playoff berth, still a heady situation for the Dukes given their recent history. The July 4 win over the Diablos was particularly memorable, a significant footnote in the history of not only the Dukes but the league in which they played. The U.S. Independence Day game featured the appearance of Tim Layana, a former major league who pitched for the Reds and the Giants in the early 1990s, who had been cut adrift by the Ottawa Lynx that day. Courtesy of Kevin Shields, Layana played three innings for the Dukes before leaving for baseball purgatory in California, a life that was ended six years later in an automobile accident. I recall annoying most of my teammates by not allowing Layana to pitch that night, thinking that it would not be ethical somehow. He did, however, play the outfield where he, remarkably enough, made an error. He did, however, go 2 for 2 at the plate. After fourteen years of widespread losing, the team had an ex-major leaguer on the roster, albeit for two hours, but still it is there in the team history.

Despite the improvements evident in the Duke record for 1995, winning seven more games than they did in last year's misery of a season, they still did not qualify for the playoffs. There were obvious explanations: they could not beat any of the better teams in the Tier, losing all ten games against the four playoff teams, five in which the Dukes gave up more than ten runs, including a total of 45 runs in two games against the Sun Devils, a team that had prompted dread in every Duke team since the league began in 1982. In one of those ridiculously lopsided losses, I was behind the plate for the first time in my baseball career, watching the Sun Devils score 26 runs as we recorded four. We even conspired to fall victim to the hidden ball trick, a laughable misfortune that turned out to be crucial in a 2-0 loss. A number of my teammates managed to put in impressive seasons — Matt Dewan, the much improved Kevin Shields, Santo Vasquez, John Pole, Dan Hodge, and Rob Lorentz all hit over .300. As for the team more generally, I was pleased enough to see that the Dukes had regained its usual mediocrity, finishing with a record of nine wins, twelve losses, and one tie. As for my own effort on the field, I ended up hitting .281, a fairly decent season for a 46 year old who sometimes forgot where he was. My own personal highlight was a ball I hit at Potter that hit the top of the centre field fence. I only ended up with a double, however, when I tripped over the bag at second. It understandably got big laughs from both benches.

About baseball more generally, an historical note — Derek Jeter joined the New York Yankees in March of 1995.

The Dukes continued to pursue their usual tradition in 1996. By that point, their story could be considered a continual cliche. Despite an ever changing cast of characters, the team managed to record similar records every year, except for the occasional nightmare of a season. Dickensonian allusions excused, the best of times and the worst of times was evident in 1996. All of this started eventfully, almost predictably for a team that had made optimism and an annual change in uniform articles of faith. Courtesy of Kevin Shields, an entrepreneurial skill suddenly evident, the team managed to attract two new sponsors, Mexicali Rosa's and the Ottawa Sports Gallery, obtained new uniforms, the third change in four years, Yankee pinstripes with a emblazoned D on the chest, an outfit that would last for another twelve years as they would be worn by dozens of players. They also recruited several new players, for what seemed to be the hundredth time in the last fifteen years.

There was also the matter of yet another change in the league structure, a tiresome institutional alteration caused by continual expansion. There would be four tiers instead of three, a change that was bound to benefit a team like the Dukes who had spent several years on the cusp of respectability under the old three tier setup. There was, therefore, considerable reason for the Dukes to feel pretty good about their prospects for 1996. As they always did it seemed.

On the field, the Dukes would show yet another different look for 1996. Three of last year's regulars, well only two of them could actually be called regulars, wouldn't be returning. Two of the three, Alberta Rosario and Santos Vasquez, left the team by their own accord, the former to parts unknown, and the latter to a new team in the league, the Latinos. The other, the team's regular shortstop and sometime pitcher, at least for the one year he spent on the club, was cashiered by general acclaim. Not to be discouraged, Shields, his acumen for recruitment growing with each acquisition, came up with two quality players, Dean Gallop and Brent Russell, from the Kanata Selects and Las Vegas respectively. Dan Hodge found pitcher Mark Fournier at work and Brian Denton arrived from the Rebels. Gallop and Russell looked great in pre-season practices and Fournier and Russell could pitch. Finally, the addition by subtraction thing was coming out on the right side for the Dukes it seemed. There was still the annual debate among Dukes as the direction the team should take in 1996. It was the usual stuff, all very boring and predictable, about who would play where and how often. Would only the best players play and what about everyone else? It was a debate that had been conducted every year since the team was founded and it had not been and would likely never be resolved. As usual, despite attempts to provide the team with sensible, if not secure direction, I would quickly find out, as I usually did, that the everything would proceed on a trial and error basis and could never be determined prior to the opening of the season.

The Dukes did not win their first game of the 1996 season until the sixth game, a 9-0 pasting of the Indians, after which they won five of the next six games. Game three was a highlight, no matter what was to transpire over the rest of the season. The team's misfortunes were tranquilized somewhat by the prospect of a game at Lynx Stadium, a last minute change in the schedule which brought all sixteen Dukes out to the game. It was a perfect Saturday afternoon, sun high in the sky, a professional baseball diamond laid out in the grass like some childhood fantasy, the empty stands the only indication that real professional ballplayers weren't playing. While the Dukes went down to a defeat, it was a perfect game on a perfect day in the perfect place. The game itself just didn't seem that important although I personally encountered some controversy when one of their base runners bounced off me during a play at first base. He was a guy who looked like he was fifteen. I remember him getting up from off his backside to challenge me to a fight. I laughed. He didn't. And we didn't fight either.

In game five, a 3-2 loss to the Bandits, another curious development befell a team that seemed to have a history of them. That game was disrupted by the sudden resignation of team general manager Kevin Shields, his exit precipitated by some pre-game foolishness about uniforms, as well as the expected exit of Dean Gallop, his excuse an apparent lack of playing time. Petulance and the dangling conversation became the order of the day for a team that looked close to capsizing.

Before the next game, the 9-0 thrashing of the Indians, there was a considerable discussion of who would be appointed, if not sentenced as the next team manager. Not that a Duke manager had much to do anyway; decide who starts, decide who sits, and then decide when those riding the pine will would into the game, if at all. I remembered thinking that that was all there was. I remembered facing some unmistakable facts, as trivial as they seemed sometimes. The team had not had coaching signals for three years and even when we had them, nobody paid much attention to them anyway. Pitchers usually decided when they took themselves out of the games, if in fact they did take themselves out of the games. Fact was the role of the manager, important to some teams, was an unfortunate afterthought on the Dukes. Who would want, much less volunteer for, a job that nobody wanted anyway, its sole qualification it seemed the ability to endure dirty looks and sometimes more direct manifestations of disapproval? It had long been a problem, a team divided it seemed between those who think that winning was more important than ensuring that everyone played and those who thought otherwise. It had been that way for every Duke team manager since John Robertson, league and team founder, took on the job in 1982. His successors, myself, Doug "Little General" Bristow, Brian Bradley, Mike Malette, and, for five games, Kevin Shields, all faced the job with equal dread, some praying for only nine players to show up at any game and others just hoping for rain. In fact, the most successful Duke teams, were accomplished much by either limiting the size of the roster, thereby risking the occasional default, (This has never happened in Duke history.) or by limiting the number of players that actually played, thereby attracting the wrath of those players who didn't play. Either way, there were, or could be, problems.

Despite such anticipation, the 1996 season had to be considered a disappointment for the Dukes. Playing in a tier in which the team should have been more competitive and in fact may have had high hopes of being so, they only managed to match their nine win total of 1995 in two more games. On balance, the two major additions to the team, Brent Russell and Mark Fournier, were more than adequate compensation for the three

Dukes who left. While the team wasn't in the habit of being routed, a habit to which they unfortunately became addicted in 1995 when they saw the opposition score at least ten runs on multiple occasions, they still lost five games more than they won, a fate that the team virtually guaranteed by losing the last five games of the season. On paper, particularly in the major statistical categories, the 1996 edition of the Dukes was seemingly a better team than the one it had succeeded, although it should be noted that each improvement was apparently countered by slippage somewhere else. On offence, they were slightly better than 1995 although four players, Dewan, Malette, Pole and Russell, the latter two threatening several team hitting records, were responsible for over half of the team's output. In fact, remove their production from the lineup and the team average would have been below the dreaded Mendoza line. The pitching, which was supplied by five individuals, including the two new players Fournier and Russell, was more than serviceably good but the fielding, long the Duke curse, was again at the root of their difficulties. In fact, someone calculated that almost half of the runs scored against the Dukes in 1996 were the result of their old friend, the fielding error. There was, of course, no need to point out that the Dukes did not qualify for the playoffs for the third consecutive season. Reminding people of that fact was admittedly becoming tiresome.

Although I took over the field manager's job yet again, I hurt my leg, in fact I may have broken it, when I was hit with a baseball fairly early in the season. As a result, I made few plate appearances. It even hurt to sit on the bench. On the other hand, at the team barbecue at the Hodge hacienda in Stittsville, I received an award from the team, a framed plaque of my number on which was inscribed "In appreciation of fifteen years of dedication and wisdom", a comment about which there may not have been universal agreement. I was more than surprised. I wished my brother John had been there.

After not making the playoffs since 1993 and not winning more games than it lost since 1992, the Dukes practised their usual modus operandi, hoping to reverse an ignoble tradition. Kevin Shields, who returned to manage the 1997 team after resigning partway through the 1996 season, convinced most Dukes that radical therapy was required. Apparently equipped with a mandate to clean house, the team decided to seek the resignations of longtime Dukes Jack Livingstone and Peter

Low who had put in 15 and 13 seasons with the Dukes respectively. It was a definite break with team tradition. After all, Livingstone was one of only two Duke originals left on the team, me being the other, and Low had more plate appearances as a Duke than any other Duke but myself. While Livingstone did not respond to his forced retirement, taking it with apparent stoicism, Peter Low did not take the news well, a reaction with which I was genuinely concerned. While it was a team decision to sever relations with Mr. Low, it had been left to me to give him the bad news. In addition, another Duke veteran Malcolm Larabie, who had graced the team off and on since 1985, was leaving for the more relaxed atmosphere of the Braumeisters. The Braumeisters, who specialized in only playing guys over 35 years old, did not try to recruit either Livingstone or Low, a pity I thought at the time.

With four players definitely gone, 1996 part-timer Brian Denton, a switch-hitter who was amiable enough to carry the affectionate nickname "Little Hurt" without complaint, being the fourth. With the enterprising Shields in the lead, the Dukes managed to recruit four new players: three of them, Jean Bastien, Kevin Donnelly and Dave Sneyd, came from the defunct Razorbacks, and a fourth, Scott Newton came from the Yankees, for whom he had won seven games last year. And for a couple of weeks, Bert Heffernan, formerly a catcher for the Seattle Mariners and more recently the Triple A Ottawa Lynx, was prepared to play for the Dukes, now that his professional playing career seemed over, a surprising development engineered by Shields. Mr. Heffernan, who left to play ball in Taiwan within ten days or so, the Duke pipe dream of having another major leaguer on the roster evaporated as quickly as it had emerged, was able to attend one practice and play one exhibition game for the Dukes before he emigrated. I remember taking throws from Heffernan at second base during that practice and later during that exhibition game. At first, I admittedly had trouble holding on to his throws. They seemed to arrive much more quickly than I or any of my teammates were accustomed, causing some of us, if not all of us to have difficulty catching the ball. Mr. Heffernan, who was one of the most affable of teammates, actually apologized and undertook to "take a little off" his throws in the future.

I remember contemplating the ironic peculiarity of having an ex-major leaguer actually apologizing to us for not being as feckless a fielder as the rest of us. Then there was the exhibition game against the Braumeisters. Heffernan played three or four innings, made two plate appearances in which he dribbled a ball out to the pitcher, later explaining that his timing was obviously off. His second time up, Heffernan hit a ball that landed in the parking lot thirty feet beyond the centre field fence at the Kinsman Field, which may have been the largest fields in the city. Not surprisingly, it was one of the longest home run I ever saw in any NCBL game, regularly scheduled, playoff or exhibition game, rivalling a 1993 homer hit by a Duke opponent at the Brittania Park that landed on a softball diamond that was maybe 450 feet from the plate on the diamond on which we were playing. The other memorable aspect of that home run, which was hit by a guy named Denis who played twenty years later in the same slow pitch league in which I ended up playing, was that it was hit off a pitcher who was attempting to intentionally walk him.

Then, almost as quickly as they had developed, things started to fall apart. Off the field, there were indications of future financial strife when the team could not make its first league fee instalment without dipping into the team's equity, an unprecedented move in the team's history. On the other hand, the regular season was about to begin. For the most part, things were looking up for the Dukes, as usual I guessed. Within six games, in which they split games, including a win over the newly constituted Sun Devils, no longer the nemesis featuring players with names like Dean, MacKay and O'Connor, but a completely new team comprised of youngsters, including a young lady named Shannon playing second base.

Over those six games, however, a number of curious things transpired. Kevin Shields, unwilling to abide criticism of his handling of the team finances, quit his job as team general manager and then three games later, resigned as a player, joining former phenom Matt Dewan as a team alumnus, the latter quitting the team after four games. New Duke Dave Sneyd hit four triples in three games. Brent Russell not only had four three hit games but stole home twice, got ejected from two games, including one in which he was thrown out on purpose, tried to score from second base on a sacrifice fly and makes a putout at first base from shortstop. Aside from Russell, John Pole had another terrific season, producing his second consecutive twenty hit season. There were, however, several unfortunate developments. There were a number of games in which three or four Dukes spent entire games on the bench, the unfortunate consequence of having seventeen players on the roster. On the other hand, they played the last two games of the season with only eight players, any chance they had at the playoffs gone.

Despite the machinations and the melodrama, the expectations and the effort, the enthusiasm and the ennui, the Dukes once again suffered a less than inspiring fate in 1997.

Still, they were one win better than they were the previous year. It was the fifth consecutive season in which the team had lost more games than it won and the fourth consecutive season in which it had failed to make the playoffs. After sixteen seasons, more than 375 games and almost 80 players, I again had to face the fact that the team would continue to struggle to survive the mediocrity of almost all its history.

As for my own season, I thought that I continued to confound time and my presumably bemused teammates by not sufficiently embarrassing myself on the field to merit a permanent spot on the bench or somewhere off the team. Despite an ungodly age, having turned 48 years old before the season started, limited playing time, and a return to the responsibilities of field manager, a role that was once again thrust on me, I almost returned to the hitting glories of more than a decade past. One small footnote. I managed to produce two base hits, including a double off the fence at the Sportsplex, from the right side of the plate, the first time I successively switch hit in over ten years.

Before the 1998 season, I was to contemplate, as I often did, the destiny of the Dukes. To offer up an advertisement regarding the performance of the 1998 Dukes, the cover of the team magazine for that year featured a Duke cap posed ominously on a memorial in the Pinecrest Cemetery. I expressed that wonder in the usual review of the 1998 team in that humble publication. Was the team in fact cursed? Was there something about the team that brought out the dark poltergeist in everyone who played on it? Were there bad vibes in the bats, a whammy on the catching equipment, phantoms attacking the fielders' gloves? Was the team doomed to failure by tradition, a tradition that goes back to the first game the Dukes ever played, doubtless a five error loss to some team or another? Was there, and has there always been, an identifiable, measurable quality to playing for the Dukes that inevitably leads to losing? Was losing bred into the bones of the players? Were the Dukes fated to self-destruct every year, a kind of permanent winter of a team that transforms grand expectations, first into disappointment, then into regrettable failure, then laughable farce, and finally into some sort of twisted optimism for the next season. Were the Dukes that good at losing, that good at being bad. After all, they compiled only four winning campaigns out of the sixteen seasons they played and lost fifty more games than they won over that period. Existential pretensions aside, did any of this matter?

So every year, it was the same script, the predictable, well rehearsed, well documented descent into turmoil, mediocrity and sometimes worse, the name Dukes synonymous with ruin. In 1998, it was the worst of times, the Duke curse turned up to the max, on another roll into some sort of nightmare of perpetual defeat. Melodramatic? Perhaps. Overstated? Maybe. But when a team wins only three out of twenty four games, even a species as thick as a sportswriter would eventually conclude that something profoundly wrong had happened, and kept on happening. Hell, this was a team in desperate need of therapy most of the time, a team that endured half a dozen of its players resigning in one way or another before and during the season itself, one of its players even packing it in after the first inning of a routine blowout loss, leaving a bewildered team with eight players to hold an equally bewildered opponent to less than three converted touchdowns. Players were leaving with certain predictability. Previous luminaries like Dave Sneyd, Kevin Donnelly, Ken Watson and Matt Dewan were gone before the season even started while veterans Neil Corriveau, Scott Newton, Mike Malette, Rob Lorenz, and maybe their best player, Brent Russell were either leaving the team outright or had announced that their playing time would be seriously compromised by job commitments and the like.

Expectations were predictably dim before the season started. Team finances were a shambles, the sponsors were gone, and there were only enough players to field half a competitive team in 1998. Of course, there were new players, it was a necessity every year it seemed. Don Little, who had been managing and playing for the Tier II Yankees, signed on with the Dukes early, adding another arm, a ton of enthusiasm and a musician's resume to the mix. Through Little came Rich Bellefeuille, another former

# INNINGS

Yankee who ended up quitting after playing sixteen games. Two University of Ottawa students Bill Guna and Matt Stiermann, joined the team after it had played two games while Chris Wallace, a veritable Roy Hobbs like player who went on to not only pitch but to lead the Dukes in practically every offensive category joined from the Lynx. He basically replace Brent Russell who left the Dukes on the same day Wallace arrived. And finally, my brother John returned after six years on the sidelines, the Duke need to avoid several forfeits the main purpose of adding this particular prodigal son to the roster. John appeared in nine games in each of the 1998 and 1999 seasons before finally disappearing into Duke history, a history for which he was largely responsible.

The Dukes won four of the twenty four games it played in 1998, a record as sorry as the 1994 season in which they won only two of twenty one games since the two of their 1998 wins were by default. As was the case after so many Duke seasons, the reasons for the team's nearly perpetual failures, big and small, were almost self evident. In 1998, the explanatory, however contradictory, was simple. The team had too many players and then it had too few. More than two dozen players participated in at least one game for the Dukes in 1998 although the Dukes had to scramble to field at least nine players and sometimes eight players for most games they played. Only three players made at least 50 plate appearances for the Dukes in 1998 while in the previous year nine did. The previous year, twelve players appeared in at least fifteen games while in 1998, only seven players did. In addition, of those players, only two were actually on the team the previous year. There, of course, was other evidence. In 1997, of the 17 players who appeared in at least one Duke game, only two were not regulars. In 1998, of the 25 players who appeared in at least one Duke game, ten could not be considered regular Dukes, including one guy whose three plate appearances were so regrettable — he faced nine pitches and swung and missed all of them — that his statistics were never recorded. And on top of that, four regulars actually quit during the season. As expected, lack of stability in the lineup spread to lack of stability on the field. In 1998, the Dukes used ten pitchers, including yours truly, six catchers, six first basemen, seven second basemen, five shortstops, six third basemen, and an incredible thirteen different outfielders. No wonder the team had no focus. It was literally all over the field.

At the plate, it wasn't much better. The team's three top hitters from the 1997 squad either didn't return or quit during the season while the team's two best hitters on the 1998 team, at least according to batting average, were recorded by the two oldest players on the team, including yours truly who hit .361, my first .300 batting average in a decade. There were games to remember: ejections, plenty of humorous errors, including a spectacular three base error in which Dan Hodge knocked over two of his teammates in pursuit of an infield pop, several shutout losses, including one in which the team could not score a single run despite producing ten base hits, and, in a fitting coda to the season, suffering their second default loss of the season when a skeptical umpire did not allow two guys holding cricket bats to temporarily play for the Dukes, reasoning that they were not likely to be on the Duke roster.

# ANOTHER CHAPTER UNFOLDS

**A**gain, like a repeated cliche, there was little doubt, much less argument, that the previous year's edition of the Dukes was, and there is no reason to equivocate, a bad team. After all, the Dukes won only three of 21 games in 1998, three games, one win and two losses decided by default, a record for futility that barely avoided the ignominy of the two win Dukes of 1994. It was clear, as clear as it has been practically every year since the decade began, that significant changes would have to be made to keep the Dukes respectable, status that seemed to skip Duke fortunes every second year or so. With the 1998 team a shambles, on resuscitation for most of the year, it would take an effort, maybe even an extraordinary effort, if not dumb luck, to even field a team for 1999. On the other hand, there was the matter of the team's expected, if not long overdue demotion to Tier IV, where the living was supposed to be easy, if not easier. With the team headed for Tier IV, a recreational paradise which would not require the team to recruit better players, just more players. On that issue, the recreational nature might well facilitate the return of most of the twelve players who finished the 1998 team as Dukes, even though only six players showed up for the last Duke game of the 1998 season. On the other hand, that number alone was probably an illusion, illusion being a significant part of team tradition. The team had used 25 players during the 1998 season; guys were on and off the team like it was a moving bus. During the season itself, ten Dukes had left the team, including one who had tendered his resignation while he was actually on the field during a game. And to place an appropriately existential touch to the entire mess, there were those six loyalists who bothered to show up for the last game of the 1998 season.

The 1999 recruiting drive began with a simple premise. The team had been consigned to Tier IV. That might make it easier to attract players, players who might want to play for a team that would not lose most of its games. After all, there was something less than inspiring about participating in a baseball game in which your team is down by a dozen runs before your turn at bat and most of your teammates look like they were playing on medication. But, on the other hand, if you think you may actually have a chance at avoiding such embarrassment yourself twice a week in a number, you might want to give the good old Dukes another try. In any event, that was the general idea. Of course, it didn't quite work out that way. Team reconstruction was not going to be that easy. Of those twelve players who could be said to be on the team on the 1998 team at season's end, only six could be counted on to return. Four Dukes, including longtime Duke John Pole, just wouldn't be back, while two others, four year veteran Neil Corriveau and 1998 phenom Chris Wallace, were offered better deals elsewhere in the league.

Of course, there was always the team's past to secure its future. With almost ninety former Dukes wondering around the city mumbling to themselves about previous Duke calamities, surely there must be three or four luckless ex-Dukes masochistic enough to return to the scene of previous tragedies. Mike Malette, the longtime Duke catcher who hardly played at all in 1998, said that he would rejoin the team. Jack Livingstone, who had played for the Dukes for fifteen years before being ingloriously dumped prior to the 1997 season, was ambivalent but not negative about the proposal. Dave Taylor, one of the best players in Duke history, was miraculously located and was almost immediately enthusiastic about the returning to a team for which he had played for four years in the early '90s. The team then added Craig Bagshaw through Dan Hodge, Dave Barnett through Don Little, Matt Jacques through Chris Gray, and James Tanguay through Mike Malette.

After a couple of indoor sessions and an accidental exhibition game against an unidentified Tier II team, original plans started to go south. Expatriate Duke Jack Livingstone decided that he'd rather preserve his Duke memories rather than tarnish them any further. A guy named Matt Jacques showed up at one practice, gave general manager Dan Hodge some money and then disappeared. Craig Bagshaw, who had shown some promise in the team's exhibition game, decided to do something else. And then, just to punctuate the dread with which team management was now anticipating the coming season, Mike Malette, counted on to bring some sense of order to the catching position after the misadventures of the previous year, fell off ladder or something and would be out for the year.

Suddenly, the team had only nine players with which to lose. Again, the team was in a search for players. Help was, however, on its way. After enduring several years of running the psychodrama known as the now defunct Lynx, a team which had a history of laying regular beatings on the Dukes, not to mention on themselves, Jeff Lefebvre, who was an actor and would go on to great fame when he become public address announcer for the Ottawa Lynx in 2002, joined the team. Then two unknowns, Brick Billing, he of the theatrical Christian name, and Kerry Franchuck, after inquiring about playing vacancies at Valiquette's Sports, agreed to terms. They now had twelve players, which as it turned out may not have been enough. There was the unfortunate Brick Billing, who even though he had his own catcher's equipment, proved to be not much of a catcher, a revelation that allowed the team to discover that Dave Taylor was probably the best catcher the team ever had. Problems emerged. One of the outfielders didn't seem to have played the game before, standing alone out there as if he were trying to hail a cab. He was gone after three games. The team's shortstop was fifty years old and two of the three remaining infielders were over 35.

In a frightening reflection of last year's disasters, the Dukes open the 1999 season by losing its first two games by seven and eleven runs respectively. They then surprised themselves, not to mention the rest of the Tier by reeling off four straight wins, during which Dan Hodge, James Tanguay, and Dave Taylor all hit home runs, a player named Matt Massey, late of another defunct team the Thunder, arrived to play shortstop and start a great season at the plate, Don Little struck out eleven Hurricanes in six innings, and the Dukes were above .500 for the first time in several years. The Dukes fell to below .500 within ten days and the Dukes continue to add players. A guy named Tim Roszell arrived from Carleton University and Area 51 to play an elegant first base and produce three hits in his first game as a Duke, finishing the season with a .429 batting average. Another new Duke, an acerbic individual named Jon Buckland, arrived to manage three hits in his first game, including two doubles, to beat the Braumeisters.

Around the same time, I had likely the most productive run of my baseball career since I was in little league. Over three games, I reached base ten consecutive times, on seven hits and three walks. I finished the season with a batting average of .375,and led the team in stolen bases. Although it was probably one of my three or four best seasons in my twenty odd seasons with the Dukes, I was most proud of the fact that I struck out only once in my 53 plate appearances, a record that I probably had never equalled on any baseball team, in any baseball season I ever played. In addition, I was in the middle of the only triple play that I believe the Dukes ever pulled off in the stored history of its fielding prowess up until then. On reflection, however, I admit that the umpire probably was being charitable in giving us that third out at first, it being later suggested to me that he may have just wanted to see a team accomplish that rare feat. It was also curious that no one on the other team bothered to contest any of the three out calls.

Players continued to come and go on the Dukes as the season wore on. Billing, Franchuk and Barnett all retired from the team while an ex-national junior team star named Kevin Collins joined the team for two games, during which he recorded six hits, including three doubles and a triple, and a walk in eight plate appearances. When I proposed to recruit him for the remainder of the season, one game and the newly established consolation round playoffs, Collins declined. I was later told that Collins did not particularly like baseball, despite the fact that he was probably the most talent player ever to play for the Dukes, aside of course from the two ex-major leaguers who graced the Dukes for a game each several years ago. The Dukes completed the season by failing to make the playoffs for the sixth consecutive season, edged out by the Sweat Sox due to a run differential calculation. But still, they lost four more games than they won in 1999. Ahead lay the consolation round playoffs, a round robin reward for mediocrity instituted by the league that year. In the consolation round, the Dukes swept to their championship of any kind in their eighteen year history by winning five out of six games. There were several individual Duke highlights during the consolation round worth recounting. Jon Buckland, who became the first Duke in history to hit for the cycle in a single game, led the team in hitting, producing eight hits in sixteen at bats, among them three doubles, one triple and a home run. He and Dan Hodge drove in ten runs. There was also Dave Taylor, who, although he did not manage a hit, walked twelve times, stole ten bases and scored thirteen runs in the six games. Finally, I continued to hit pretty well in the consolation round, managing two doubles, including one that hit the top of the left field fence at the Sportplex. With their winning record in the consolation round, the Dukes completed the 1999 season at the .500 mark, the first time they had done that since 1992.

Unlike previous seasons, going into the 2000 season, the predictable Duke optimism, which was always regarded as an illusion, was not misplaced. The 1999 team was obviously better than most of its recent predecessors. It had been fortified by newcomers like Jon Buckland, Matt Massey, Tim Roszell and James Tanguay. It had been improved by the return of catcher Dave Taylor. It had propelled itself to respectability, a state that the team had punctuated by sweeping through the consolation round with almost ruthless and rare for them efficiency. This was a team that had hit .317 in the regular season and .326 in the playoffs. The Dukes hit nine home runs in the 24 games they played in '99, a big number for any team, an astounding number if you were the Dukes. On the top of that, they had six players who could actually pitch without embarrassing themselves. Although general manager Dan Hodge's characterization of the team as a "powerhouse" was a trifle exaggerated, even for him, there was no doubt that this team was good and was expecting to get better.

Over the winter, it had become apparent that the only significant loss to the team would be outfielder Chris Gray, who had decided to pursue his political ambitions in Toronto rather than Ottawa. To replace Gray, original Duke Steve Williams, who left the team in 1990 to establish and then run the younger and more competitive Expos for a decade, agreed to return, finally relenting after seven or eight years of listening to annual Duke entreaties. Through Williams came pitcher Dan Valiquette, a veteran of a number of NCBL teams going back almost fifteen years. In addition, Williams was able to deliver hitting and slick fielding Peter Williamson, an another Expo emigre. John Allaire, a former Junior A hockey player, media consultant with connections to the Liberal Party, and local musician of some repute, joined the team part way through the season to hit .389 in only five games before an injury cut short his debut season with the Dukes. Then, there was Sylvain Chauert, an associate of Mark Fournier, maybe the best pitcher the Dukes have had since Rob Power was striking out 70 guys a year back in the mid-80's. The Dukes had looked good going into the 2000 season, not only good but better, the only bummer a late James Tanguay announcement that he wouldn't be bringing his team leading bat back to the team for 2000, his work schedule too chaotic to allow him to commit to the team. Still, with four new high quality players, two being bona fide pitchers ready to step in, maybe there wouldn't be a problem. And as it turned out, there wasn't.

There were a couple of developments in the first three games of the season that were indicative of the future of the team over the next three months or so. In the opening game, Sylvain Chaubert held last year's champion Knights to five hits and nine Dukes authored base hits in beating them 11-2. In the next game, they outhit the expansion team Rockets 8-4 but still lost 5-3 due to a flurry of Duke fielding miscues. They then beat the Sharks 10-7 behind new team ace Chaubert who had taken over on the mound after starting pitcher Dan Valiquette was ejected for hitting three Shark batters in one inning. The game was also significant in that the team welcomed the arrival of Pete Williamson who managed three base hits and a walk in four plate appearances and accepted seven fielding chances at second base without making an error, quite an achievement for a team that seemed addicted to them. By the time the Dukes reached the halfway point of the season, they had won four games, lost four games and tied one. Their ninth game was significant in a particular way, at least from my perspective. With only seven Dukes available to start a loss to the Coyotes, my teenage son Ben was pressed into service to play the outfield with me. Although Ben struck out twice and walked once against fearsome Coyote pitcher Bob Brooks, he doesn't look badly out of place. The rest of the season is a revelation, a nine game undefeated streak awaiting.

In constructing their nine game unbeaten streak, the Dukes manage a number of memorable moments. James Tanguay, last year's MVP, returned to play in the first game of the team's nine game unbeaten streak. Aside from Williamson, who finished the season hitting a Duke record batting average of .439, easing my own 1986 record by four percentage points, Allaire, Hodge, Little, Massey, Roszell, Tanguay and myself all started to hit a ton, most of the named finishing the season by hitting more than .300 with two players, Williamson and myself hitting over .400.

# INNINGS

Chauert, Fournier, Little and Valiquette all made for a formidable pitching staff, likely the best the Dukes ever had. Although the Dukes ended up compiling the best regular season record in their history, winning twelve and tying two of their eighteen games, almost edging out the regular season champion Braumeisters for top spot, misgivings proved prescient as the playoffs approached. While Dave Taylor was back from injury, John Allaire was gone for the rest of the season, a ruptured achilles tendon the culprit. And Tim Roswell was still recovering from a couple of cracked ribs suffered when he was hit with a pitched ball. Any trepidation that the Dukes may have felt before the playoff round robin began proved to be prescient as the Dukes went down 5-3 to the regular season champion Braumeisters. Predictably, it was errors that did the Dukes in: a botched defence of a bunt with runners on first and second and a subsequent wild pitch led to three of the five Braumeister runs. In addition, the final Braumeister run, which was scored on a clean single, might well have been prevented if Dave Taylor's spectacular throw from centre field had been handled. The game was also memorable for another distressing footnote. The Dukes played without five regulars: the gone for the year Allaire, the still injured Roswell, Buckland, Massey, and Tanguay. The Duke hadn't lost in more than two months and now they were on a losing streak.

The Dukes then righted themselves somewhat with a thrilling, nerve rattling, final at bat win over the Raiders 8-7. The heroes were many, including most particularly Matt Massey who awoke from what for him was a mediocre season with three hits, including a double and a home run, four runs batted in and the winning run in the last Duke at bat courtesy of a Dan Hodge single. They then went on to engage in an entertaining 5-5 tie with the Knights. It was a game in which Little pitched brilliantly at times against a team that knew how to hit. It was a game in which Little did not give up an earned run, all five Knight runs scored after a Duke miscue. There were four in all, which one allowing an inning to continue when it should have been over. They had all sorts of chances to win the game but didn't, runners left on base, runners picked off and runners thrown out at the plate all contributing to the missed opportunities. The Duke season was over, its end anti-climatic when their scheduled opponents, the Crickets, had the game cancelled for reasons unknown. However, a Knight win the previous evening robbed that game of any relevance. The Knights won the tier championship and the Dukes, who had just had their best season in their history, didn't.

Like last year's team, the 2000 version of the Dukes was a serious improvement over its immediate, if not all of its predecessors. This time though, it was the pitching that propelled the Dukes to the best record in its history, the offence almost identical to the offence of 1999, any differences lost in the minor shuffling of statistics. As always, the Dukes had next year to think about, their expectations understandably high for once.

It was to be their twentieth season as a team, an anniversary so fraught with possibility that only a half bright sportswriter could have overlooked an anticipation of triumph. These were the Dukes for god's sake, a founding member of the league in which they had floundered so brightly for the past two decades. The league in which they had played was also twenty years old, only the Dukes, the Sweat Sox and the Sun Devils were survivors of the original six teams that formed the league in 1982. The Dukes had played so many games, used so many players, and endured so many disappointments that fortune owed them something, even if it was a halfway decent shot at the winning that had eluded them for so many years. And the 2001 Dukes, after recording their best record in their history in 2000, would be deserve it too. Duke optimism, a curiously stubborn trait that has been two decades in incubation, would finally be vindicated. A couple of old guys, particularly myself, could retire, and the team could forget about next year until next year. It didn't happen. It didn't happen at all as things started to fall apart for the 2001 Dukes before last year's World Series was done. Team most valuable player, Peter Williamson, announced in early October that he would be returning to Oakville. John Allaire, who had hit a ton after he joined the team midway through last season, said that an injury he incurred last year may be serious enough to keep him out this year as well. And Tim Roszell, the young professor who hit .375 in 2000, moved somewhere other than Ottawa. It was not even Christmas and the Dukes were faced with the unenviable prospect of replacing three of their best players.

As in most previous years, efforts to recruit new players were spotty, if not entirely ineffective. Nothing seemed systematic, everything just happenstance and fortune. I ran several thinly attended indoor sessions in the winter that yielded little in the way of new players. A promising infielder named Chris came and went. James Tanguay, who had been the team's most valuable player two years ago but had seen his playing time cut dramatically by job commitments last year, said that his attendance was unlikely to get any better in 2001. Jon Buckland, another star of the resurgent Dukes of 1999 who hadn't played much last year, was evasive about his status for 2001. On the other hand, Mike Malette, who last saw action as the team's catcher in 1997, was apparently ready to return. There were, however, more significant problems ahead. The core of the team's pitching staff, Mark Fournier and Sylvain Chauert, started a new Tier III team called the Chiefs and their arms would therefore be the core of that team's pitching staff. In addition, the new franchise was to be sponsored by the Ottawa Towing Co., much to the ire of tow truck driver extraordinaire Dan Hodge. Courtesy of Steve Williams, the team had a line on a couple of ex-Expos and there was always the newly installed league website, a remarkable advance over the old-word-of-mouth, tryouts-at-Potter days, when there was nothing too organized to bail out those unambitious teams who needed players but didn't have a dependable way to sign them.

Foreboding seemed the appropriate state of mind when the Dukes assembled, after much disassembling in the offseason, for their first game of the year. Only six Dukes, included the repatriated Mike Malette, bothered to show up to oppose the Rockets, a team resplendent in bright and white uniforms provided by their new sponsor, that pinnacle of sophisticated dining, Hooters. Nevertheless, the Dukes did manage to field nine players for the game, having convinced the Bell brothers, who had been hanging around the Trillium Park contemplating suicide, to play outfield, while a third volunteer, a Hodge buddy named John Tremblay, played third base, all to avoid a forfeit. It was a strange game otherwise. Tanguay pitched for the first time in two years, Dave Taylor went back to his original position in centre field, and, just to place a nice nostalgic touch on proceedings, a 52 year old, namely yours truly, played shortstop. While the Dukes did lose the game, they weren't demolished, a strange optimism having set in, even though the team wasn't sure it actually had nine authentic Dukes on the roster. Three days later, even though they lost again, this time to the Coyotes and their fearsome pitcher Bob Brooks, the Dukes were fortified by the Gagnon brothers, Carl and Sebastien, as well as another Gagnon, though unrelated, named Paul. Jon Buckland also showed up in his only appearance of the year. There were several footnotes and post scripts to the game. Seventeen Dukes strike out in a six inning game; Dave Taylor disappears after the game for the next three months; Paul Gagnon is cashiered two days after the game for having a bad attitude about his playing time; and both teams had to deal with a dog which had been wandering about the field until the fifth inning or so.

As if to celebrate the arrival of another new Duke, Kemptville's Fred Hazelton, another ex-Expo who eventually proved to be a flawless fielder, a consistently productive hitter and a player of such unrelenting hustle that he was eventually and unanimously nominated for team's MVP honours in his first year with the team, the Dukes finally managed their first win of the year, a 10-3 victory over the Sweat Sox. Hazelton eventually proved to be another Roy Hobbs personage, a star who was so shy that teammates thought he was hiding something. Over the next couple of months, the Dukes managed to win only four games and tie one game to finish the season with an unfortunate record 5-12-1, a considerable fall from the 12-4-2 count of last year. In losing those ten losses that finished the 2001 season, the Duke team and individual Dukes contributed a number of memorable moments to a history full of them. The Dukes lose two of the games by default, hit six home runs, including two each by Seb Gagnon and Matt Massey, and suffered the most ignominious defeat of their 20 year career, collapse to the extreme of the word in going down to the eventual Tier champion Crickets by the ungodly score of 28-5. We played with eight players that game, my son Ben in right field where he made a spectacular catch to keep the Cricket run total to less than thirty. I was behind the plate for all 200 of Dan Valiquette's pitches and all 25 Cricket base hits, a catching assignment to again complete playing all nine fielding positions, the Cesar Tovar career record. I also stole home in one game and made an error in another when I fielded a ground ball and then somehow lost the ball in my jersey.

Like they did two years ago, the Dukes salvaged their dismal regular season with a fairly respectable consolation playoff run. But unlike two years ago, they didn't rampage through the consolation round. In fact, they didn't even win it but the effort was there, a final record of 4-2 a fair indication. And there was plenty of suspicion, all four of their wins by one run. They won their first playoff game when they manage to nail ex-Duke Malcolm Larabie, who was playing for the Braumeisters, trying to score from third on a Matt Massey wild pitch in the bottom of the seventh inning. They then beat the Sweat Sox 6-5 after coming dangerously close to defaulting the game, eventually convincing a bystander named Warren DeLima, who for some strange reason was sitting in the stands at Brewer Park wearing baseball cleats, to step in for the Dukes. Matt Massey and I shared the catching duties, Don Little gets the pitching win, the Gagnon boys produce four hits between them, and Steve Williams produces three hits. To keep the curiosities intact, the Dukes follow one 6-5 win with another 6-5 win over the Hurricanes. Dan Valiquette struck out ten for the win, including the last two with the bases loaded in the top of the seventh inning, made two superior fielding plays, and laid down the bunt of the year to pave the way for Jeff Lefebvre to drive in the winning run. The Dukes then closed out the round robin portion of the consolidation playoffs by edging the Sharks 13-12. Despite two hit performances by six Dukes, they needed another two out play at the plate in the bottom of the seventh inning to keep the Sharks from tying the score.

In the finals, the Dukes lost two straight to the eventual consolidation round champion Braumeisters, 7-3 and 8-7 defeats, the latter punctuated by a perfect night from Braumeister power man Pete Chaput who included a home run among his four hits. One interesting sidebar. For maybe the second game of the season, all but one Duke showed up for that last game, an occurrence so unusual that I had difficulty remembering how to fill in the lineup card. We closed out the season, out but not down. It was another year in the books and another series of explanations, many of them quite familiar. Rather than ruminate about them, comparing these statistics to those statistics, it was really quite simple, as it usually was. Most of time, as it often was in the past, the Dukes just didn't have enough players to go around. Consider. Of the 24 players that appeared for the Dukes in 2001, nine were not even on the roster. The Dukes defaulted two games, played half-dozen games with a non-roster player in the lineup, and played only a handful of games with more than nine players on hand. In fact, only six players were able to show up for more than half the games. In summary though, the Dukes, with their consolidation playoff run, retained their respectability, again.

As for my season, I hit .300 and made only one error while playing five positions. And my son Ben played another game for the Dukes.

Assessing the last couple of Duke seasons, mired in consideration of the usual myriad of statistics, I started to think about the meaning of such data and the changing nature of their meaning to the game of baseball. As I indicated earlier, I have long been fascinated with baseball statistics, an early obsession with baseball cards the likely origin of that particular compulsion. Baseball cards usually displayed each player's career numbers, sometimes even included a player's minor league stats, their comprehensiveness limited it seemed to me by the space available on a baseball card. That is the reason I guess that I am profoundly old fashioned about baseball stats. I am rooted I guess in some outdated conception on how we should measure the performances of individual baseball players. To me, there is no game so dependent on the durability of its statistics as baseball. I mean, Ted Williams hit .406 in 1941, no matter how many times one attempts to rebut the value of that particular statistic. Give me batting average, hits, runs, runs batted in, home runs, maybe doubles and triples, maybe stolen bases but probably no more. All of these are splendid enough things, aren't they? I mean, when Casey Stengel said that you can look it up, I don't think he meant that you needed a doctorate in quantum physics to do just that.

I remember including an article regarding the overall issue of statistics in one of the Duke publications back in the early 90s. It was likely prompted by the increase in the types of baseball statistics offered by various sports magazines at the time. In the article, I noted that baseball was a curious game. It seems to keep stats on everything, no matter how apparently inconsequential. Want to know how someone hits against left-handers during night games on the east coast? You can probably find out. No other sport, save perhaps for the crazy minutia of most Olympic sports where hundreds of seconds are measured out like rosetta stones, is as concerned with statistics as baseball. No matter how hard they try, football, basketball and hockey couldn't come up with 37 categories of data if you lent them a new laptop and four guys in tech support. And that doesn't include the pitchers who have another 35 categories of information on which to contemplate their fates.

The most prominent statistic that has emerged over the past few years among aficionados of baseball academics is called *Wins Above Replacement (WAR)*. It is an attempt by the sabermetric community to summarize a player's total contribution to their team in one, easily digestible statistic. (Sabermetrics is the empirical analysis of baseball, especially baseball statistics that measure in-game activity. Sabermetricians collect and summarize the relevant data from in-game activity to answer specific questions. The term is derived from the acronym *SABR*, which stands for Society for American Baseball Research, founded in 1971. The term was coined by Bill James of "Moneyball" fame.) *War* is all-inclusive and provides, at least according to most observers, a useful reference for comparing players. Basically, *War* is an estimate of the value of one player to the team compared to a player who might replace him. As indicated, it expresses that value in terms of the wins that a particular player brings to the team. While supporters of the statistic claim that it is not as complicated as one might think, it does require a significant amount of information to calculate, requiring a complex comparison of the individual player's performance to the performance of a replacement level player in a number of different categories. Predictably, the career leaders in *WAR* are roughly, if not precisely consistent with the career leaders in most other statistical categories. According to a publication called "Baseball Reference", the top five career leaders in *WAR* are Babe Ruth, Cy Young, Walter Johnson, Barrie Bonds and Willie Mays while the top five in the 2018 season were Mookie Betts, Mike Trout, Jacob deGrom, Jose Ramirez, and Max Scherer. The players in both rankings are hardly surprising.

If I was ever in a position to calculate a *WAR* for each one of my Duke teammates, which I would never even consider, the possibility of assigning such comparative values to individual players anathema to team spirit. Besides, given the lack of hitting and fielding prowess of the Dukes over the years, the appropriate definition would be "*Wins Below Replacement*" or "*Losses Above Replacement*" — whatever generated the least resistance from players who were hardly appreciative of being measured by such a method. As for the statistics I compiled for the Dukes for the last million years or so, and for the entire league through most of the 1980s, I usually settled on sixteen or seventeen well known hitting categories, running the gambit from games played through plate appearances, at-bats, runs, hits, and the like to on-base percentage, fourteen well known pitching categories from game appearances through wins, losses, innings pitched, earned runs and the like to earned run average and the batting average of the opposition, and finally, as added in the mid 1990s, fielding statistics, the least popular and often ignored.

However, as I found out in my first few years of collecting statistics for the league, individuals and teams generally have different criteria for judging what constituted hits in particular. It is easily recalled, at least by me, that at least one team with which I was familiar was in the habit of regarding anytime anyone reached first base as a legitimate base hit. Everything, hits, fielder's choices, walks, errors, and dropped third strikes were all scored as hits. As a result, there were exaggerated batting averages beyond normal comprehension. There was no deception intended in such cases, no score keeper malfeasance intended to inflate batting averages and such. Instead, it was apparent after at least one team handed in score sheets which had pretty well every player in their lineup hitting well over .500 that something was amiss. It was quickly determined that the people doing the scoring had no idea as to what they were doing. In those early days, however, the compiling of individual statistics, beyond the scores of the games themselves, was not a high priority for most teams, my brother and I the sole custodians it seemed of such information, sorting it out from the game score sheets themselves. It was eventually concluded therefore that in the first couple of years of the Ottawa Recreational Baseball League individual statistics, particularly batting averages, should have been regarded with some skepticism.

Despite an array of baseball statistics, whether hitting or pitching statistics, one statistic that has always gotten the cold shoulder from both the fans and the players it seems measures fielding performance. It has been, and remains I suppose, the black sheep of the world of baseball statistics, consigned to purgatory by embarrassed players and unappreciative fans. While fielding percentages usually appear in most baseball publications, I have always assumed that few readers payed them much attention. After all, it is predicated on making errors, hardly the kind of information to be passed around in public. When I introduced fielding statistics to the Dukes sometime in the mid 1990s, it was admittedly controversial, with most of my fumbling teammates voicing expressions of complaint. Speaking of fielding statistics in particular, I calculated and included them in the individual team publications for over a decade, precipitating some controversy and general ennui among my occasionally disgruntled teammates, many of whom ignored any indictments of their error prone ways. I noted later that the team seemed to have discontinued calculating fielding statistics as soon as I left the team. I was not surprised.

After another less than mediocre season, I managed, with a literary shrug of resignation, to attach the term "nowhere men" to the Dukes of 2002. I noted that after twenty years and more than 450 games, the Dukes entered the new season with the same desperate optimism they have shown almost every spring since that first year back in 1982. The last year, they were compelled to start that season without the core of their pitching staff and two of their best hitters. It certainly showed in the standings as the 2001 Dukes won seven less games than they did in 2000 and failed to make the tier championship playoffs. They did, however, regain some measure of respectability with another good showing in the consolidation playoffs. But that was the previous year. For 2002, they would face their usual dilemma. They would need players, particularly pitchers, especially after four year veteran pitcher Don Little announced that injuries would prevent him from returning. Over the winter, the Dukes were able to sign pitcher Matt Girard, who would turn out to the staff workhouse on the mound, and Mathieu Bougie, who would provide the team with one of its fastest players since John Pole was in his mid-20s. Those additions, as well as the return to full time status of John Allaire, Dave Taylor and James Tanguay, all of whom missed significant time in 2001, gave the team some cause for expectation for 2002, even if it was relatively fleeting. In addition, another newcomer arrived to play seven regular seasson and five consolation games for the Dukes, a Matt Girard referral named John Mitchell who hit over .400 and then disappeared. Maybe hope was too hopeful a word.

While the Dukes finished the season with a hapless six wins in twenty games, they did manage to split their six consolation playoff games. Despite another year of evident misfortune and mediocrity, there were a number of positives. The Dukes remained a relatively cheerful lot through most of the season with no distractions to speak of. For the first time in six years, they batted over .300 as a team, led almost inevitably by John Allaire and Fred Hazelton who together accounted for a third of the team's offence.

In fact, both finished the regular season with regular breaking batting averages, Allaire at .519 and Hazelton at .472 with Allaire easily bettering the mark of .439 set two years ago by Pete Williamson. Together, the duo produced 53 base hits, the most by any two Dukes in a season since Dick Bondy and I combined for 57 hits in 1986. On the other hand, the Dukes allowed the opposition to hit .342 against them, despite the blameless efforts of Girard, Massey and Valiquette. As the primary indication, the Dukes allowed almost as many unearned runs as earned runs. In other words, it was a typical Duke season.

As repeatedly indicated, optimism has been, and always will be one can assume, a bedrock Dukes characteristic. It seemed bred in the bone, sown in the seams of the uniforms, forged into the bats. This is a team, though rooted in a tradition of perpetual losing, which faces every spring with the resignation of hope that it will not lose, that this year it will actually win something. True, it has not won anything in its twenty odd year history in the National Capital Baseball League. Still, despite such a longstanding jinx, it has struggled mightily in the last two decades to improve its prospects. Every year, it is the same thing, a constant cliche of prognostication. More players, better players. To that end, the team has been witness to wholesale changes of unequally frequency, having used and sometimes reused over 120 players in that history. They have changed uniforms, six or seven times although not at all in the last six years. They have had great players, they have had nearly great players, they have had mediocre players, and have had players who couldn't hit a baseball with a canoe paddle. They have had older players, they have had younger players, and they have had players who sometimes appeared to be deceased. They had had players who stuck around for ten years. In fact, yours truly had played for all 22 years and others played for a week and a half. They have had every variant of player and personality. They have battled, they have prodded, they have embarrassed themselves and they have had nervous breakdowns. They have attempted everything short of an exorcism to improve.

It was no surprise then that activity prior to 2003 season was frenetic. Last year, they had shown flashes of excellence, particularly at the plate, but had won only six of twenty games and had split six games in the consolation round playoffs. They could hit. The Dukes had a team batting average of over.300 average with players like Allaire, Sebastien Gagnon, rookie John Mitchell, and Steve Williams all hitting a ton. But the Dukes had difficulty holding their opponents to fewer runs than they scored. The Dukes also made their usual quantum of errors, allowing between two and three unearned runs a game, the stellar efforts of the pitching trio of Girard, Massey and Valiquette often going unappreciated. Duke management, principally Seb Gagnon and myself, spent the winter searching the league website and running session at Grounders looking for prospects. They knew there would be holes to fill. John Mitchell was quitting outright, James Tanguay was looking at a work schedule that would limit his playing time, and Fred Hazelton was considering not returning. We did, however, manage to attract several quality recruits. There was former Dodger draftee and Valiquette relative Marc Andre Legace and his buddy Martin Poitras as well as NCBL veterans Marc Landry from Tier I and Mike Glustein from Tier II. Not only were these guys quality recruits but two of them, Legace and Glustein, were proven pitchers. Despite the usual high expectations, cracks started to show. Original Duke Steve Williams, who played a stellar outfield and hit .342 in the process, retired to play softball. The Hazelton and Tanguay situations remained unresolved as the season opened.

The Dukes, now managed by Seb Gagnon, opened the season by losing four straight games, a period during which Fred Hazelton played his last game for the team and Landry, Legace and Glustein proven their worth, the latter two both on the mound as well as at the plate. In fact, Legace was already hitting over .500, with two doubles, a triple and a home run to his credit. It took the fifth game of the season for the Dukes to win their first game, a 4-3 defeat of the Knights, a game in which I returned to the team after contemplating retirement for a couple of weeks, the prospect of only playing occasionally finally making an impact. For the record, I make eighteen plate appearances during the ten games in which I made the lineup, my third fewest appearances since I spent a lot of time riding the pine in 1989 and 1996.

The Dukes won four of the next five games, a streak during which individual Dukes made memorable contributions in the team history. In a 12-2 victory, Marc Andre Legace struck out 18 Crickets in recording the first no hitter in the team's history, his next game a pedestrian one hit win over the Hurricanes. After that record breaking Duke performance came two others in a 17-11 loss to the Raiders. Not only did three Dukes hit home runs in a single game, Glustein, Landry and Massey doing the honours, but two of them, by Landry and Massey, were hit in succession. The Dukes managed to get to .500 with a late season win over the Rockets, a game in which I returned to manage the team for sixth time in my 22 years, replacing five previous managers, Bristow, Bradley, Malette, Shields, and lastly Seb Gagnon. All of my predecessors lasted less than one year each at the helm before giving up the glamour of a negative cash flow, little playing time, and complaints and dirty looks for less lofty pursuits. I managed to guide the team to two more wins and a tie to ensure both a playoff berth and a record that was above .500 for the first time since 2000. In our last game of the season, a tie with the Sharks, I recorded the 250$^{th}$ hit of my Duke career, a total that is almost 90 hits more than the second more prolific hitter in Duke history, John Pole. Although the Dukes did manage to make the 2003 playoffs, completing a record of nine wins, eight losses, and one tie, they eventually lost to the Crickets in the quarter finals. It was the last game of the season, however, that resounded long after the players left the field. Although the official score of that last game was recorded as 14-3, the actual count was much higher in favour of the Crickets. It was a game in which the Dukes gave up fourteen runs in three innings, the Dukes were left to play with eight players after at least one Duke left the game before it was over, and the umpire was persuaded to call the game in the fourth inning further to my request, the unofficial score having the Crickets scoring more than three converted touchdowns.

# THE EMERITUS YEARS ARRIVE

The winter between the 2003 and 2004 seasons was easily identified by that well known Shakespearean observation. It was a winter of discontent. For me, it was profoundly personal. In early February, I underwent cardiac surgery, an event that I thought was almost certainly going to change my plans for participation in Duke fortunes for 2004. I was not oblivious to the possible Duke future after the disappointment of the 2003 season. Sure, that year's team had a hole here and there but when you hit over .300 as a team and have seven of your regulars hitting close to or over .350, good prospects seem inevitable. Add four dependable pitchers to the mix, including one that seemed practically unbeatable, at least until his arm fell off toward the end of the season. It was then that the Dukes were closer to the top than they had been for several years. Still, despite all those upbeat possibilities, it all fell apart in the first round of the playoffs, a fate that was punctuated when the Dukes got massacred by the Crickets in the final game of the season. It was clear that the whole team had become less than the sum of its parts.

While the Dukes had fallen well short in the field in 2003, there were familiar problems off the field as well. Several Dukes, most particularly the veterans who had spent the season riding the pine, weren't happy. It reminded me of the 1989 season when there were in reality two Duke teams, the one with players who played and the another with players who didn't. In the fall, I decided, as one of the veterans consigned to the bench for much of the 2003 season, that maybe the time again was right for a radical change. The idea was to split into two teams, just like 1989 when one group formed the Expos in the then competitive division of the league while the rest of them remained the Dukes in the newly formed recreational division. Clearly, there were at least half a dozen players on the

2003 team, specifically the guys who played all the time, who could play in a higher tier in 2004. To that end, Seb Gagnon was already working to recruit players from higher tiers. As for the allegedly less talented Dukes left behind, they would see their playing time increase. To fill any vacancies on that team, the current Dukes could turn to the old Dukes, of which there could be over a hundred still wandering around the city exchanging old stories. Within a month, long time Dukes Dan Hodge and John Pole, who had not graced the team for two and six years respectively, were re-signed. Steve Williams agreed to come back while Matt Massey, Dave Taylor, Jeff Lefebvre, Matt Girard, James Girard and myself were enthusiastic about the changes, the prospect of more playing time at the heart of the matter. As for me, with my heart surgery in February, it was evident that I would be sidelined as a player in 2004, if not permanently. Then, against my better judgment, I agreed to return as general manager and coach, after receiving a call from the NCBL Commissioner regarding his concerns that the Duke franchise was in danger of folding. In that context, a slew of former and current Dukes, including Pole, Hodge, Massey, Lefebvre, Girard, Tanguay, Taylor, Williams, Valiquette and unexpectedly, Gagnon, his plan to form a separate team gone, Matt Bougie, team MVP Legace, and three time Duke and former Braumeister Malcolm Larabie all said they would be returning. Within weeks, however, Williams and Hodge dropped out. Throw in newcomers the Milano brothers, Gagnon buddy Pat Groves and former Diamondback Dan Remigo and now there were sixteen Dukes and a bench full of optimists.

After several surprisingly well attended practices, the Dukes opened their season by starting their treadmill to oblivion, a losing streak that would extend to twelve game. At that point, there were only six games left to avoid the infamy of a winless season. The streak included two defaults, both of which prompted me to actually consider taking the field, a proposal that so unnerved my teammates that they wouldn't play if I played. In addition, the team played three games with only eight players. By the time the first week of July rolled around, that summer was starting to look like winter. Despite mounting evidence I had developed some sort of baseball Alzheimer's, my winless record as team manager being offered into evidence, I was to discover that I couldn't be fired no matter what the team record, the reason being that no one else would want the job. Further, the sixteen player roster had shrunken significantly, with Larabie, Legace, Taylor, one of the Molina boys, and Hodge all either announcing their resignations or going AWOL without explanation. However, despite several whimsical prognostications about a winless season, the Dukes finally won a game, an inevitability one supposes. So when that win came 9-5 over the high school all stars that were the Tigers who ended up winning seven games that season, the Dukes are suddenly serene, so relaxed that they end losing their last five games, to complete 2004 with a record of 1-17, the worst in the team's 23 year history.

So how bad was the 2004 team, the last team on which I had any specific role, aside from being the scorekeeper. There was never any doubt in my mind that the 2004 team would have routed the 1994 and 1998 teams, the only statistical competitions for "bum of the year" award. The 2004 team, despite its disappointments and its delusions, had better hitters, had better fielders, and better pitchers than either of those woeful ancestors. The simple fact was that while the 2004 team was a profound disappointment, the competition against which it was compelled to play had improved dramatically. The league was better, the team wasn't.

As for myself, I was determined again to transfer management of the team to someone else, anyone else. As for playing again, I was determined about that too. After all, there was little doubt that after the spectacular despair of the 2004 season, there would be major changes, both on and off the field in 2005. While the 2004 team was never as bad, at least relative to some of the unfortunate Dukes teams that had preceded them, the pathetic assemblages of the 1994 and 1998 as already noted, the growing competitiveness of Tier IV of the National Capital Baseball League required that either the Dukes improve significantly or actually contemplate extinction. While a dim future had a certain existential allure, Duke management, which had fallen into a partnership between a reluctant Seb Gagnon and myself, was actively looking for an answer. In fact, we were looking for a saviour, someone to shoulder the burden of reconstructing a Duke team that was badly in need of reclamation. Neither of us wanted the job. Gagnon was more interested in playing than managing and I was tired of only watching others play.

Not that change would be a problem for the Dukes. Throughout their history, a well chronicled history that predates the establishment of the league itself, the Dukes have been defined by change. The evidence was persuasive. The team utilized over 125 players in its 23 years and had only three or four players who had been on the roster for more than three years. There was, therefore, no concern, when Gagnon and I offered management of the team, if not the team itself, to Dave Barras, a pickup basketball colleague of mine who I had been pursuing as a player for the Dukes for years. Barras, late of the PMA Panthers, Diamondbacks and most recently the Yankees, was serious enough about the Duke offer to basically assemble an entirely new team within weeks, adding five former Dukes, including Marc Fournier, who hadn't played for the Dukes for four years, to a core of Yankee, Panther and Diamondback alumni. It had become obvious almost immediately. The team wasn't being changed, it was being replaced. It would be the most fundamental alternation of the team since the 1990 season when the Dukes were divided into two separate teams. It would also be the first time in the team's history that a Robertson would not have something to do with the team's fate.

With the agreement of manager Barras, who was demonstrating ambitions for the Dukes that had not been seen for years, I attended several practices in an effort to demonstrate that I was still capable of actually playing for the Dukes. Surrounded by new Dukes with whom I was unfamiliar, there being only three or four players with whom I had ever played. For the first time since I played fastball, more than thirty years ago, I was a rookie, the alienated new guy, just trying to make the team.

Although I thought I had showed enough in practice to qualify as a player for the new Dukes, it was obvious, at least to me, that the players who Barras had recruited were likely to be in the lineup long before I got a chance at it. In addition, most of the new Dukes seemed to know each other although I didn't. By way of contrast, I knew only six of the thirteen full time Dukes in 2005. Although I was dressed in a Duke uniform for the first game that season, a 5-2 loss to the Hurricanes, I did not get into the game, little more than a spectator, even score keeping duties having been handled by some other bench jockey. I actually do not recall the precise circumstances of my fall from grace but before the second game of the season, I turned in my uniform. Although I was not formally notified that I was being released from the team, it was clear, at least to me, that I had been dropped. I handed in my uniform, my only request that one of my former Duke teammates receive my jersey number, the revered number seven. I seem to recall that prodigal teammate Marc Fournier, who had not played for the Dukes for five years, claimed it.

I did not dress for another Duke game until sometime in 2007, by which time while I did not have a uniform, I did have a number of t-shirts, baseball pants, and cleats as the appropriate costume for an emergency player. In the intervening years, team manager Barras kindly gave me an authentic Dukes baseball cap from some minor league team as a memento of my more than twenty years as a Duke, now apparently complete.

Despite the infusion of a number of new and presumably better players, the Dukes finished the 2005 season with a humble 6-10-2 record and a 1-2 record in the playoffs, for which every team in their Tier qualified. As there usually is, there were both highlights and unfortunate events. Mike Pignat became the second Duke in history to throw a no hitter, Hugh Cairns and Marc Fournier hit two home runs each during the season and the playoffs, and in a strange historical footnote, four of the five Dukes who dipped below the Mendoza line of a .200 batting average in 2005 played for the ill fated Dukes of 2004. Of these four, only one of them played for the Dukes in 2006. There was something strangely symbolic in such statistics. Within three years of talking over the team, the Dukes of 2004 were just a memory, that at least until 2007 when I came back for four plate appearances in two different games. That was the year the Dukes finally won a Tier championship.

For reasons that I cannot recall, while the Dukes posted a record of ten wins and eight losses in the 2006 regular season but lost in three in the first round of the playoffs, I did not take note of any of the Duke accomplishments that year. I did not produce a magazine that year, for the first year since 1982, my only acquaintance with my alum mater the occasional review of the league website. Earlier in that year, I pursued a tryout for another team in Tier IV, the Sharks. Although I thought I performed quite adequately during that tryout, a practice that must have attracted more than fifty candidates, I was told that while I would be a valuable addition to the time, both at the plate and in the field, I was just too old, the manager observing that he did not think that having a player in his late forties on the team was a good idea, no matter who that player was. While I did not offer a rebuttal, I could have told him that I was not in my late forties. Fact was that I was 57 years old at the time.

I definitely did not have a place to play that spring. The previous summer, my stay on the Dukes being limited to one game, a game in which I did not play, I participated in a few games in a Kanata slow pitch/lob ball league on a team whose name I cannot remember and may not have ever known anyway. It was an open men's league, meaning that anyone over eighteen years old could play. Accordingly, the ages of the players, at least on the team on which I found myself, varied widely. My guess though was that no one on the team was my elder. I had never previously played slow pitch/lob ball, my acquaintance with softball, that variant of baseball player with a larger diameter ball, being limited to fastball, where the ball is thrown underhanded as fast as possible by a pitcher using a windmill windup. On the other hand, slow pitch or lob ball is a modification of the same game but the underhanded pitch must arc on its path to the batter and is therefore thrown much slower than in fastball. In slow pitch, there are ten rather than nine players on the field at the same time, there is no bunting, no stealing, no advancing on passed balls. There are walks although no hit batters. There are strikeouts although a two strike foul ball becomes a strike, the strike being a swing and a miss, a foul ball or a pitched ball landing on a square that is much larger than a conventional plate. There are a number of other rules particular to slow pitch, including a limit on the number of home runs each team can hit. Finally, a regulation softball game requires seven rather than nine innings.

In any event, I played several games for one of the Kanata slow pitch teams, remembering only one of the games, during which we were absolutely clobbered by a team which seemed to be exclusively manned by young men with impressive biceps and a propensity for the long ball. I cannot recall how I played although I think I may have made a couple of laudable plays in the infield. I don't remember the reasons for my short stint with the team nor can I remember the name of one of my teammates, none of whom I ever saw again.

For reasons that have long escaped me, I found myself playing two games for the Dukes in 2007, at their request I assume. It appeared that the team was undermanned for games against the Hurricanes and against the team that had declined my services the previous season, the Sharks. After three years of not playing, I found myself playing second base, bewildered but steady enough to generate a hit, a run, a run batted in, a sacrifice bunt, in the two games, no recollection of a fielding error in either game. I was not invited to play any additional games for the Dukes that season although I did return to publishing the annual Duke magazine, my main motivation not recalled. I did, however, had found a great picture, an action photograph of Duke Mike Pignat, for the cover. A former member of that team told me several years later that I should have attended the game when they clinched the Tier championship with a 14-5 victory over the Hurricanes. Only three players from pre-2005 Duke teams appeared on that championship team, the only championship in the team's 36 year history.

For most of that summer, however, I also played for a nameless fast pitch team that played out of the Bell softball diamonds in Bells Corners. The minimal age was either 40 or 45 years old with no maximum. Fast pitch was the third type of softball that I had played. The game was almost identical to fastball except that the windmill windup of the pitcher is restricted to a shoulder height back swing. Although the ball came in hard to the plate, it did not come in as hard as it did in fastball. As a result, there was more hitting in fast pitch. As far as I can recall, our team, which may have been called the Knights although I am not quite certain, broke even. Again, I cannot recollect the names of many of my teammates on the Knights, remembering a Ross, a Bob, a Geoff, a Dick, an Ian, a Ray, and maybe a Ralph although I cannot be sure of that or the names of any of the guys I just enumerated. I played the infield, mainly third and second base, and was probably acceptable in the field and productive at the plate.

The guys on the team were different in demeanour that the those of the Dukes, their contrasting age the principal explanation. There were few, if any players on that team who took themselves seriously, meaning that team management, either a guy named Geoff or a guy named Ralph, did not have to deal with the cavalier head cases that every manager of every recreational ball team sometimes has to deal with. Most of the guys were generally relaxed. One reason for the relatively loose atmosphere of the Knights, or whatever the team was called, was the tradition — I was never sure whether it is a tradition or a rule — of allowing every player who shows for the game being inserted in the lineup. Everybody got to hit, a custom that would have made my latter years with the Dukes much less dismal than they eventually turned out to be. There were few disputes or arguments. In fact, when I gently disagreed with an umpire's call at second base in one of earliest games, I was almost ejected from the game. The other difference, of which I took notice, was that the older players, the ones playing fast pitch with me, discussed woman more often than the younger players. Women and home renovations were particularly popular among the older guys.

After only playing the two games I played for the Tier IV champion Dukes in 2007, I was ambiguous about my status for the 2008 team. When it was not actually made clear, I did have the impression that if I decided to show up at the Duke games, they would put me on the roster, without a guarantee of playing time. The 2008 Dukes opened the new season with approximately the same roster as the 2007 club, the addition of catcher Andrew Hierlihy the major change, but with new uniforms, teal and white uniforms with expensive new caps. I was looking forward to perhaps enjoying more than a modicum of playing time, maybe even returning to the seasons when I may have seen action in half the games. But I hurt my knee early in the season and had to go on injury reserve and then went on to contribute significantly to the team's fortunes by not playing in many of its games, ending up with only one hit in five at bats. I did, however, drive in two runs. I also continued as the team statistician and scribe, publishing another edition of the team's magazine, which may have been the ultimate objective anyway. I really didn't mind being of such service, even though I suspect few of the Dukes actually read the magazine, except for the player biographies and maybe the statistics. I may have always been delusional but I have enjoyed producing the annual publication, thinking for some mysterious reason that I was pursuing literature, literature of an inferior quality but literature nonetheless. As for the Dukes of 2008, they duplicated the record of the previous season winning ten games and losing eight. But they lost in the Tier finals to the eventual champion the Rockets. One can assume that the new uniforms did not have the effect that was intended by team management.

That same summer, I rejoined the fast pitch team that was still playing in Bells Corners. The team had added a few new players, two of whom turned out to be pretty good players. Like the previous year, I cannot recall how the team, which I still thought were called the Knights, performed that year although I am pretty certain that we did not win anything. I recall that the team's only weakness, if indeed we had a weakness although I guess we must have been so afflicted since I don't think we won any sort of title, was a fairly pedestrian pitching staff, our sole pitcher being a man who hardly threw fast enough to frighten anyone. Like most details of my history with that team, I am uncertain as to the results of the games or most of the players on either my own team, the Knights, or any other team in the league for that matter. But I do remember that in general, it was a fairly enjoyable season. I cannot recall, however, one particular episode that could have contributed to that impression. I think that year was the last season for the fast pitch league that played at the Bell diamonds. Next year, I would find myself playing for a slow pitch/lob ball team, also called the Knights at the same location.

Over that winter, having finished putting some time in for the Dukes and at the same time for the slow pitch team the Knights, I started to contemplate my own athletic oblivion. I was now almost sixty years old, past middle age into my emeritus years, playing a game for the barely post-adolescent, hoping not to embarrass myself. Golf, an endeavour I had abandoned years before, began to look pretty good by comparison, at least to me. On the other hand, I knew that time was unarguably kinder to baseball players than it is in most other sports. Sure, other sports have had their Gordie Howes, their George Blandas, but that was a long time ago, Tom Bradley notwithstanding. Age, particularly in athletic pursuits where guile alone will not carry one alone, is one albatross from which there is no escape. Slap on the blades in your mid-forties and continue to play with whom you do not share a generation, and more often than not, you'll end up sucking on nitroglycerine spray like they were Popsicles before long. Check out a bunch of over forties playing basketball in a school gymnasium and pretty soon you will be hear the wheezing in the parking lot. Football? Forget it. A game of touch with some twenty year olds and you might as well call a chiropractor. And tackle? No one has ever played adult tackle football unless of course you want to call it rugby.

So it may come down to baseball as a last refuge of the faded jock. Isn't baseball the sport in which a 45 year old pitcher named Bartolo Colan is still playing in the major leagues? So age alone is no automatic ticket to a few extra years in athletic purgatory. It does, however, give some pause to those whose advancing years make them obvious candidates for retirement. The dilemma, whether to finally withdraw from the game or tough it out as the immovable object at the end of the bench, is only relevant for those playing at the competitive level. Presumably, if you are playing mixed softball after work or are playing with with over fifty types, this quandary would not apply. Presumably, you could continue to fumble around the ball park without regret, your disappearing skills lost in the similarly faded skills of others. But still, there is no real guidance as to whether you keep playing, even if it has become obvious that you should not.

Although I cannot be absolutely certain, I think I continued to play for the Knights in 2009. There may have been a number of new players on the team but fewer teams in the league, fast pitch it was suggested to me becoming less popular. Again, as in previous years, I cannot recall any of the details of any of those games and whether I contributed in any positive way to the team's fortunes that year although I probably did. On the other hand, my tenure with the Dukes was somehow enhanced despite signs that my career with that team or any other team in the NCBL for that matter was becoming a distant memory. I got into four or five games that year, usually if not always as a late inning replacement, appearing at the plate seven times, my most appearances since 2003, the last year I played on the Dukes while managing the team at the same time, squeezing fourteen plate appearances out of a season in which most of the starting players did not abide playing the bench for any reason.

Dave Barras, who had taken over the Dukes in 2005 after I have given up the team after running it for 22 years, and had then guided the team to a title in 2007, announced his resignation as manager after the 2008 season. Succeeding him for the 2009 season was one of the team's most valuable players, the affable Larry Pawelek. Manager Pawelek showed remarkable resiliency in leading the Dukes to more regular season wins than they had compiled for almost a decade. They were able to win those eleven games that year without the full time services of Duke stalwart Hugh Cairns, who hit almost .400 in his five seasons with the Dukes, and part timer Stephane Ouellette. In addition, workhorse pitcher Steve Rumleski left for another team. Manager Pawelek responded by recruiting Steve Brown, who affected the aura of that fictional natural Roy Hobbs, and NCBL veteran John Mendonca, who would go on to play for the Dukes for five years before starting his own team, the Orleans Lynx. Strangely and surprisingly, a team that won eleven out of eighteen games and hit .329 as a team, lost in the first round of playoffs to the Coyotes. As for me, not only was I provided with more plate appearances than I had had since 2003, I recorded an on-base percentage of .857, reaching base six of the seven times I got to the plate. Although I did not know it at the time, although I probably should have, I was now prepared to put in my long overdue last appearance on the Duke roster.

While I did not absolutely know it for a certainty at the time, there was an unavoidable irony in the title of the lead article for Duke Edition XXVI of Baseball Ottawa, the annual publication on which I and for a time my brother John had laboured so valiantly since 1983. That article was entitled "Sudden Departure". Perhaps I knew or should have known, whether by osmosis or some other trick of cognition, that the 2010 season would my last as a Duke and my last in the National Capital Baseball League. In the gallery of player chronicles, I had described myself as an extremely engaged fan, my actual occupation on the team that of team clerk and statistician, duties that allowed, if not required me to produce Duke Edition XXVI, a 97 page booklet that contained the usual elements, an article on the season, the player biographies, player and team statistics regarding the season, and as a final decorative touch, eleven articles on various aspects of baseball in general and the Dukes in particular, easily the most comprehensive volume I ever produced for the team. I had attempted to resign from the team during the season itself but manager Pawelek had talked me out of it, suggesting that I was an important member of the team, without mentioning the valuable statistical and journalistic services that I was supposedly providing. I relented, manager Pawelek's ingratiating comments to me having the desired effect. I went on to pretty well all 22 regular season and playoff games that the Dukes played that year, amassing two hits and a sacrifice bunt, about which several of my teammates complimented me. I had six plate appearance that last season, retiring with an official career batting average of .303 on 255 hits with 194 runs and 168 runs batted in. When I finally packed it in, I held several Duke records, including career hits, runs and runs batted in. I have no idea as to my current standing in the annals of Duke career hitting. I played on the Dukes for 28 years.

The 2010 Dukes were a team that had won 15 games during the regular season, the highest number of regular season victories in its history. They had finished the regular season a mere one game behind the regular season champion Sharks. This was a team that had outscored its opposition by 56 runs over the regular season and had hit .313 as a team with eight regular players hitting almost or over .300. Even more impressively, this was a team that had recorded an unusually low earned run average of 3.75 during the regular season. This was therefore a team that had the credentials to take back the Tier title it had first won in 2007. It seemed preordained.

It was going to happen. Problem was that it didn't. The Dukes went down in two straight games to the Black Sox.

It was not as difficult as I thought it might have been to face the next spring without a Duke team to even consider joining. With a slow pitch team to play on now, the Knights of the West Ottawa Slow Pitch Association having been established to replace the fast pitch league that had folded. The league played every Monday evening, two games of seven innings each, scheduling that was much more convenient than the NCBL schedule which spread the games out over the entire week, Saturday excepted. As far as I knew, the league was limited to players who were 45 years old with two or three exceptions, meaning that suddenly, after toiling for years with teammates who were half my age most of the time, I was playing with contemporaries, a happy circumstance that somehow brought the recreational game back to me. I played the infield most of the time, usually at third, sometimes at second. I found most of my teammates quite affable, knowing some of them from my old fast pitch team, including the manager, a guy named Geoff. The team also featured two brothers who had played for the Dukes, albeit for wildly disparate periods. They were Steve Williams and his brother Bob, the former having played for the Dukes for twelve seasons, including the team's maiden season of 1982, while the latter had played only one game for the Dukes, also in that maiden season of 1982.

I played for the Knights on Monday evening for several years without memorable incident, not a particularly surprising conclusion since I did not keep any account of specific games or the team's record in general although I am fairly certain we did not take the championship of the eight team league in any of those years. Two years later, I joined a mixed senior league that played every Tuesday morning at the government RA Centre on Riverside Drive. The rules of that league were fairly similar. The minimum age was sixty years old and each team had to play at least three women on the field at the same time. There was a wide variety of players. There were several excellent players, some of who I recognized from the West Ottawa Slow Pitch Association, and several players who were not nearly as proficient, some who could barely catch or throw, some who could barely run, and some couldn't hit. Each hitter was allotted three pitches per plate appearance, pitches that were thrown by someone who was playing for the team that was batting. There were curious group calisthenics before the games, older women wearing catcher's masks in the outfield, women who brought muffins to the games, and players old enough to perhaps inhabit retirement homes. I only played in that league for two years, the stress on my arthritic knees and other joints damaging enough to convince me that I could not play in two leagues in the same week, my stint with the Knight replacement team called the Wildcats still taking up my Monday evenings. I later played for an over sixty men's league on Thursday mornings, also at the RA Centre. Again, my physical limitations and the fact that teams were drawn up by a new draft every year, thereby producing completely new teams each year for social reasons I was told, a process with which I disagreed. I only played one season and part of another.

For the last four years, I have played with the Wildcats of the West Ottawa Slow Pitch Association, a team sponsored by the Giant Tiger department store. The full name of the team was the Ageless Wildcats and wore stunningly colourful jerseys featuring a cartoon tiger. I have been simply the least adept player on a team that has been populated with skilled, experienced players, many of whom seemed to play slow pitch in weekend tournaments that were played all over the country. In fact, I was frankly surprised that I stayed on the roster, my talents as a player hardly comparable to the rest of my teammates. I batted last in the order and manned the catching position, generally regarded as the easiest position on the field to play. In 2017, the Wildcats won the league championship, beating perennial powerhouse the Silver Bullets in two straight games in the finals. At the season end league banquet, the Wildcats were presented with the championship trophy. For reasons that still escape me, I ended up with possession of the trophy. I suspected some sort of inside joke.

Another minor footnote. In 2016, I was asked to take up the position of "bench coach", a kind of on-field advisor to the manager, for the Orleans Lynx, a recently established team in Tier IV of the NCBL, a team which sported three ex-Dukes. Two of whom played for me in the 1990s. I thought about it for a time, went to one practice and took batting practice with a wooden bat for the first time in almost forty years. Regarding the latter, the NCBL had gradually introduced the requirement for the use of wooden bats until all four tiers were using them. I decided to decline the offer of "bench coach", determining that I had spent the last few years with the Dukes doing the job unofficially and wasn't happy about it. Further, I could not help but notice that a lot of my new teammates seemed to be recent high school graduates.

# EXTRA INNINGS AND WINTER OBSERVATIONS

**O**f all the sports I've played, there was none more given to philosophical contemplation than baseball. There was something uniquely meaningful about baseball. As a consequence, perhaps every American writer of the 20th century has taken a crack at explaining the mythical qualities of the national past time. Not to be outdone, I too could pursue the poetic properties of baseball with the serenity of frequent recall. It could explain my obligation, if not obsession with producing, for more than thirty years, an annual publication on the activities of a recreational baseball team called the Dukes. Somewhere within my annual commentaries on the fortunes of each season's team, I have always suspected that I was somehow contributing to the body of literature devoted to the meaning and implications of baseball. Occasionally, I would include observations and contemplations on various aspects of baseball, where they were relevant to anything that happened to the team during the season at hand. I included articles which, although about a number of different aspects of baseball, were usually ignored by most of my teammates, some of whom questioned the utility of inviting them to read it in the first place.

I could have I suppose referred skeptical readers to the many novels written and to the many movies filmed about baseball. I could in no way even fantasize that I was somehow connected to such literary giants like Bernard Malamud, W.P. Kinsella, Philip Roth, Ring Lardner, Don DeLillo, Roger Kahn, Pete Hamil, and former Yankees pitcher Jim Bouton who wrote the famed "Ball Four". Still, I thought it was somehow my obligation as a person who always had literary pretensions to write about issues that were important to me personally, which included, if nothing else, baseball. Aside from the literary world, there were also the many movies, popular baseball movies with major stars like Kevin Costner in "Field of Dreams" and "Bull Durham", Brad Pitt in "Moneyball", Robert Redford in the "The Natural", Robert DeNiro in "Bang the Drum Slowly", Gary Cooper in the "Pride of the Yankees" Tommy Lee Jones in "Cobb", Clint Eastwood in "Trouble With the Curve", Geena Davis, Madonna, and Tom Hanks in "A League of Their Own". While other sports, football ("Rudy"), basketball (Hoosiers"), hockey (Slap Shot"), boxing (the many "Rocky" movies, "Raging Bull") and even golf ("Caddyshack", "Happy Gilmore"), have their movies, literary and cinematic stories involving baseball are far more plentiful and far more prolific than artistic work involving other sports. Baseball was a convenient avenue through which I could pursue some sort of artistic vision, as limited as it was. In other words, it provided me with material.

There was always something profound about baseball, as if its relaxed pace, its continual civility and its contemplative nature could somehow assuage the struggles of daily life by recalling the comforts of the past. In fact, I have persuaded myself that my attraction to baseball, and perhaps the reason for my continuing pursuit of playing it all these years, resides somewhere in its connection to the past, that playing it now is too much the reminder of playing it sixty years ago, as if everything has changed but baseball which looks and feels to me as it did those many years ago. I cannot help but quote the observations of Terrence Mann, a character in W.P. Kinsella's "Field of Dreams", which seems to encapsulate my belief regarding the relationship between time and baseball.

> "They'll come to Iowa for reasons they can't even fathom.
> They'll turn up your driveway, not knowing for sure why they're doing it.
> They'll arrive at at your door as innocent as children, longing for the past.....
> And they'll walk out to the bleachers, and sit in their shirt-sleeves on a perfect afternoon.....
> And they'll watch the game, and it'll be as if they'd dipped themselves in magic waters.

## INNINGS

The memories will be so thick, they'll have to brush them
away from their face....
The one constant through the years, Ray, has been
baseball."

Although such sentiments may not stand as existential articles of faith,
I have grown to accept Mr. Mann's observations on baseball as truth and
the almost spiritual relationship it has with time. No matter how many
years I have invested in playing baseball, in the different leagues, with
the different teams, with the different teammates, it was almost as if time
stood still, as if nothing had changed and nothing ever will, one of the
few things that you can care about for your entire life. My wife Pamela
gave me a baseball autographed by Aaron Judge this Christmas. It was a
wonderful gift.

I do not know whether I will play for another year. If I do, it will be
almost sixty years since I first played for a little league team sponsored by
a local pharmacy called Johnson's Drugstore.